MOTHER DIED LAST SUMMER

Also by David W. McFadden

Mother Died Last Summer

Journal of a month-long motor tour through
Great Britain (with a side trip to France) with
my father in June of 1992

David W. McFadden

Mansfield Press

Library and Archives Canada Cataloguing in Publication

McFadden, David, 1940-
    Mother died last summer : journal of a month-long tour
through Great Britain (with a side trip to France) with my
father in June 1992 / David W. McFadden.

ISBN 978-1-77126-004-6

    1. McFadden, David, 1940- --Travel--Great Britain.
2. McFadden, David, 1940- --Travel--France. 3. Poets, Canadian
(English)--Travel--Great Britain. 4. Poets, Canadian (English)--
Travel--France. 5. Fathers and sons--Canada--Biography.
6. Great Britain--Description and travel. 7. France--Description
and travel. I. Title.

DA632.M34 2013   914.104'86   C2013-901256-7

Editor for the press: Stuart Ross
Cover design: Denis De Klerck
Cover Illustration: Shutterstock
Typesetting: Stuart Ross
Author Photo: Max Middle

The publication of *Mother Died last Summer* has been
generously supported by the Canada Council for the Arts
and the Ontario Arts Council.

 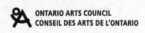

Mansfield Press Inc.
25 Mansfield Avenue, Toronto, Ontario, Canada M6J 2A9
Publisher: Denis De Klerck
www.mansfieldpress.net

FOREWORD

My son David surprised me one day, telling me he was writing a book about his and my trip to Britain and Europe. He further asked that I add a few lines about my life during my first ninety-nine years. I'm glad he didn't ask about my second ninety-nine years. That would be no easy task.

At sixteen, I joined Stelco, running a machine in the mill. A couple of years later, the office personnel decided that I could do better in the office, so I joined the payroll department. This lasted about five years. Then I was asked if I was interested in managing the stationery and office equipment department. This included the mailroom.

Like everyone else I was getting older, and I was looking around for someone to share my life with. After a few female friends, I finally found my dream girl, Elizabeth Jean Pidgeon, in 1936. This started a courtship, and we decided to marry in 1938. This marriage started a wonderful union, and we lived in perfect harmony for fifty years. Except for four years I spent in the Canadian Army.

I retired at sixty-two, and we spent a few years vacationing, moving about in various homes and, more importantly, raising two fine sons.

At sixty-five, my wife had a very serious fall from which she never fully recovered. She died in 1991 after a ten-year struggle.

I too have never ever fully recovered from my loss.

My son David helped me immensely, in 1992 taking the two of us for a trip overseas to Great Britain. We visited all the British Isles, and then crossed over to France, and all the recent battle areas.

THAT'S ALL FOR NOW. Thank you, Dave!

William McFadden
Hamilton, 2013

TUESDAY, JUNE 2, 1992

Mother died last summer, and last month I asked Dad if he wanted to take a little three-week holiday in Britain to get his mind off his sorrow and loneliness. "How about four weeks?" he said.

I took a cab to the airport today, and we picked up my daughter Jennifer on the way. When we got to the airport, there was Dad, and then my brother Jack showed up. We all went to the pub and had a merry old time drinking beer for an hour. Dad and I bought a litre bottle of Glenlivet in the duty-free shop and bade farewell to Jack and Jennifer.

The flight was miserable. No room to stretch out. Every time I fell asleep I was awakened by the guy in front jerking his seat back. Dad seemed happy though. I think he's more used to less sleep. I should add that this was not Dad's first trip across the Atlantic. The first occurred in 1975, when Mother and he took a little tour of Spain with several friends. It was not altogether a happy trip. Dad had his pocket picked, and he lost his wallet.

WEDNESDAY, JUNE 3

Poor Dad! His introduction to Britain was a gruesome one, particularly for someone as fastidiously clean as he. We got off the plane at Heathrow, picked up our baggage, and while I went over to the car-rental booth, Dad went into the men's washroom. He came out a few minutes later looking pale and sick. He said there was a huge figure of a guy lying on the floor, completely naked, no socks even, and no shoes.

"He was being hosed down with a garden hose by a couple of guys in uniforms. There was fecal matter everywhere, on the walls and even the ceiling—and a horrible stench," he said. "I couldn't tell where the smell was coming from. Oh, it was so horrible. And I couldn't tell if the guy was living or dead."

We never did find out what happened to the poor fellow. Welcome to Britain, Dad.

We picked up our Ford Escort with five-speed manual transmission and drove to Windsor. As we drove, we listened to BBC Radio 4. Dad loved this quote from the golfer Jack Nicklaus: "The more I practise, the luckier I get."

We walked around Windsor Castle, gazing at it from all angles, but decided against going in for a tour. We drove along the Thames River to Henley, where we had a mackerel sandwich with horseradish at a little restaurant on the river. We went in the church with the eleventh-century tower, famous from many "Beautiful Britain" photographs, and looked around. Then we booked a B&B at the tourist office.

But when we finally found the B&B (the directions were all wrong, and we were still very tired from the flight), the room we had booked had been taken by a travelling salesman from Edinburgh, and we had to stay in the son's room. Luckily, the son was away at college, but he hadn't left his place in very good shape. We had a lovely breakfast. The host was an unemployed architect who seemed to want us to know that he usually gets a higher class of guest. His wife was okay though. We felt a little ripped off and decided against booking at tourist offices in the future.

THURSDAY, JUNE 4

We drove from Henley to Winchester, with many wrong turns, and stopping to ask for directions. Upon arrival at this ancient capital of the Saxon kingdom, the home of King Alfred, we went on a tour of the old town and of Winchester Cathedral with the local guide, Elizabeth Proudman, who also does Salisbury walking tours.

She was pleasant, kind, patient, and well-informed. She told stories from the history of this area, plainly and interestingly, and we didn't need much of a background in history to understand what she was telling us. Her stories went back to Roman times, when Winchester was called Venta Belgarum. She showed us, high above the altar, a series of gold-plated sarcophagi which contain the remains of many ancient kings, including Canute, for instance.

We drove to Salisbury and walked around the famous Salisbury Cathedral, the one with the highest spire in Europe, the one which Prince Charles is always trying to raise money for. It was built between 1220 and 1280, but the spire is so high, and so terribly slender, it keeps threatening to collapse. I asked for Mr. Partridge, the elderly retired printer who lives in the Cathedral Close, in a house even older than the cathedral. He had taken me on a tour of the cathedral during my last visit, four years ago. And had taken me home for tea, and to show me his printing press, and the limited-edition poetry books he publishes under the imprint Perdix Press (*perdix* being Latin for *partridge*).

Sadly, Mr. Partridge had been seriously ill, but happily he seemed to be recovering. He was the same age as Dad. His wife, as well, had been ill. So we decided against bothering them.

We called on Mrs. Legg, of Wyndham Lodge, where I had stayed during my earlier trip. Mr. Legg answered and told us to come around. It turned out he and Mrs. Legg had split up last year, but Mr. Legg was still "doing B&B"— at least on a limited basis.

We took a room and cracked open the Glenlivet, which Dad had never had before, being more used to Canadian rye. I told him the famous line about scotch:

"Many have died from too much scotch and many have died from too little scotch. If you could only find the right amount you would live forever."

Dad's reply was to the point: "Well then, let's try to find exactly the right amount."

According to Mr. Legg, former Prime Minister Heath, still an MP, lives within the Salisbury Cathedral Close, and has paid £450,000 to the church for a forty-year lease. This can be seen as a philanthropic gesture, since the money will go towards the upkeep and maintenance of the cathedral and the restoration of the steeple—as well as providing one of the most fashionable addresses in the world.

I asked Mr. Legg ("Call me Peter") why Salisbury still looks as it did in the fifties, while Winchester, same size, also a cathedral city, looks very modern and spiffy. He said it's because Winchester is the administrative centre for Hampshire, while Salisbury is merely a market town. Which made sense.

He also spoke about the alleged Special Air Service habit of recruiting men to infiltrate the IRA, telling them that if they get caught they will die a horrible death and they will not be acknowledged in any way by the SAS or the British Army. In exchange, presumably, if they survive they will be on the SAS payroll for the rest of their lives.

FRIDAY, JUNE 5

A terribly cold, rainy, blustery day. We went back to Salisbury Cathedral and started exploring the cavernous interior, along with hundreds of other tourists, trying to keep out of the cold. Dad looked like a typical English eccentric in his overcoat and his Maple Leafs toque, and he did like the cathedral, but he definitely preferred Winchester. Maybe it was because Mrs. Proudman was with him when he was there. We couldn't find a guide here, because there were too many tourists. Also, a wedding was going on, or rather a blessing of a wedding since the bride—or was it the groom?—had been married before. Even Alison Fenwick, who had been my guide in the area four years ago, wasn't available; she had gone to Japan for a year to teach English.

I couldn't imagine Dad enjoying Stonehenge or Avebury in this terrible weather, so we left the area and drove down through Hampshire and Dorset to Dorchester, and then down to Weymouth.

"You wouldn't mind if it was raining, but it was bitter, terrible," said Dad, as we drove into better weather. He brightened considerably when he saw the sea at Weymouth and all the hotels and tourist places along the sparkling seafront, and the colourful and domineering statue of King George III. I told Dad he could, if he wanted, take a two-week holiday next year in Weymouth and have the tourist agency plan it for him. He said he was thinking of flying to Vancouver, renting a car, and driving through the mountains to Calgary, then flying home.

So we drove along the coast to Lyme Regis, and then to Exmouth, where we had a plaice dinner at a nice pub right on the sea, a fishermen's hangout. The bartender told us that over the past two years, four fishing boats had been lost in storms in the channel, with crews of between three and eight men in each boat. All of the men had been regulars at the pub.

Dad and I sat there for an hour after our dinner, talking about Mother, politics, life, death at sea, and so on. Then we went for a B&B in town. Dad and I drank scotch and talked excitedly about Stonehenge till all hours.

SATURDAY, JUNE 6

In the morning, I walked down to the sea and watched the fishermen going out on the tide. Back at the B&B, our host, Steve, was saying that he and his wife had the place up for sale. They were asking £125,000—but were considering accepting an offer of £95,000. He said he was a "steel erector" and had worked on the Olympia & York project, Canary Wharf, for the Reichmann Brothers. He said the workmen used to have their lunch up there on the girders, and they would wonder where the Reichmanns thought they were going to get the tenants for the building. They were right. He also said they had a big wildcat strike at one point, but were given everything they asked for, and the strike was kept out of the papers. He also said the Reichmanns had built a lavish, state-of-the-art mini-train to take the workers to the project—but it kept breaking down.

Steve, who was cross-eyed, said he grew up in Coventry, in the middle of the town, which had been rebuilt after extensive bombing in World War II. He said it was an urban jungle there. He had taken his family to Florida for holidays a few times, and had even travelled in Canada, including Toronto and Hamilton, too. But now, for the first time in his life, he was out of work. No jobs for steel erectors. The recession had hit hard. Things were so bad, he was applying for work way up in Aberdeen, Scotland. But he insisted we visit the eighteenth-century fishing village of Mavagissey, in Cornwall.

Which we did. Dad and I had a fine time, walking up and down the narrow streets and eating ice cream and Cornish pasties. I bought a couple of books about Cornwall for my daughter Alison in the local bookstore. We met a man who was one year older than Dad and we walked up the coastal footpath with him. He was a retired coal miner from Nottingham and had many funny things to say, every chance he got, and he got plenty. Dad and he got along famously. Dad was very impressed that this old codger, a widower and long-retired, travelled extensively all over Britain—and by himself. And he was so cheerful and self-contained.

We spent two hours at Mavagissey. Dad bought a

new belt in a leather store. We watched as a man came around the corner eating a huge ice-cream cone. All his friends (he was a local) started hooting and laughing at him for eating such a big cone.

He said to them: "It's not as big as the one I had half an hour ago."

We drove to Penzance and took a room at the Camilla Guest House. I spent a quiet hour as Dad had a little snooze, then we walked around town till nightfall. We considered the possibility of taking a ferry from Scotland to Norway, and then going across to Sweden, down to Denmark, Germany, Holland, Belgium, France, and back to England. Or maybe taking a ferry across to Holland, down to France, and back. It was cold. We had fish and chips. And beer.

SUNDAY, JUNE 7

We drove towards Land's End, passing the Pipers standing stones and the Merry Maidens stone circle, and a very good megalithic burial mound which much impressed Dad. We walked across a field to inspect the Merry Maidens. There were a bunch of "new age" people who seemed embarrassed by our presence. They were middle-aged, and getting ready to perform some kind of ancient Druidic ritual. They had drums and flutes. We walked all the way around the circle, then back to the car.

Just past Land's End, on the way back, on the northern side of the peninsula, I hit a rock on the side of the narrow road and we blew a tire. We changed it—Dad helping me to figure out how the jack worked—at the side of the sea and at the foot of a hill with a ring fort on top. I could see hilltop hikers through the binoculars and got to watch a pair of female hikers taking off their sweaters as the weather was warming up. Of course, they had T-shirts underneath.

We drove all along the coast to St. Ives, where we

had ice cream and walked along the beach, which was warm and sunny and thronged with people. Then we drove along to the horribly commercialized Tintagel, where King Arthur was thought to have been born, according to Geoffrey of Monmouth, the twelfth-century chronicler. In the parking lot, a fellow sold us a guide book and said Father wouldn't have any trouble on the way down to the castle because there was a four-wheeler that picked people up and dropped them off, for fifty pence. So we walked down, secure in knowing we could take the four-wheeler back up, and Father climbed the rock steps all the way up to the ancient ruins of Tintagel Castle overlooking the wild and wonderful sea. He was very proud of himself—and rightfully so. He was very cheerful, too, and kept saying to perfect strangers, "Do you feel as fresh as a daisy?" "More like a dried flower," came back one answer.

But then, when it was time to go back up to the parking lot, we were shocked and appalled to find that the guy who ran the four-wheeler had knocked off for the day. We were scandalized. The fellow who gave us the bogus information had locked up and gone home by the time we got back up to the parking lot. Father was exhausted, even though we had gone as slowly as possible, and we took several sit-downs at benches, all the way up. I wanted to leave a nasty message for the fellow, but we decided not to bother. I didn't want to upset Father too much. He was taking it all very well—but he assured me he wouldn't feel like climbing Glastonbury Tor tomorrow.

At Torrington, just over the Devonshire border, we were running out of petrol. We stopped at the Panting Billy to ask for directions to an open filling station, since it was Sunday and most were closed. We had given up trying to get our tire fixed until tomorrow. They not only directed us to an open station, but one fellow insisted upon taking his reserve tank from his boot and emptying it into our tank, to make sure we didn't run out on the way, and he wouldn't take any money for it. This sort of kindness we were to find everywhere in Britain—and sometimes the opposite extreme.

We got our fill-up, then drove west along a narrow, winding, two-lane highway. But Dad was a bit nervous, sitting as he was in the passenger seat (as I would have been in his position), and kept thinking we were about to be in a terrible accident, no matter how slowly I went, no matter how long the lineup of cars and lorries stretched out behind us. I decided that we should henceforth spend more time on the motorways, the "dual carriageways," and so on.

Meanwhile, I felt as if the spirit of Glastonbury was calling us, and although I didn't expect to have time to get there tonight, we were making good time, getting very quickly across Devonshire and into Somersetshire. There was a period of uncertainty near the town of Yeovil, where I'd been told the records of my maternal grandfather John Pidgeon's schooldays would be available, and I pulled over and got out to have a look at the map. A couple stopped their car and asked if we were lost. I told them we were heading towards Glastonbury.

They said to follow them, for they were going home to Weston Super Mare and would lead us to Glastonbury—it was on the way. I said, "But you're going south." They said no, they were going north but they had doubled back when they saw we were in a bit of trouble. "We're good Samaritans," said the wife. They were very nice people. The man stammered a little. As we followed them towards Glastonbury, we could see the Tor looming ahead in the mist. The good Samaritans pulled over, and I thanked them, and they gave me their names and addresses so I could send them a letter of thanks when I got back home.

I never did get any of Mr. Pidgeon's student records. But I do have his 1885 Bible and some very interesting but clandestine drawings of his schoolteacher. Mr. Pidgeon (he died in 1932) was a very good sketch artist and his penmanship was terrific. He had written in his book: "John Pidgeon, Blue School, Wells, May 11th 1900." He liked to write, in white ink, on black paper, and he grew up in Cardiff, Wales.

We found a B&B in Glastonbury, run by Nick and Sue Carter. We were a bit hungry when we pulled in, so Sue very kindly made us a plate of sandwiches—and a pot of tea, of course. She also gave me a book to read, from her collection of old books. "I just love old books," she said. It was called *Glastonbury, or The English Jerusalem*, by Rev. C. L. Marson (London: George Gregory Book Store, 1925 [4th edition]). I read it till I fell asleep—and when I woke up, I read it some more.

MONDAY, JUNE 8

Mrs. Sue Carter served breakfast while Clannad played on the stereo. Father loved the stereo and wanted one just like it, even though it was a fairly old model, as stereos go, circa 1977. I think it was the music of Clannad that he really liked. He also liked the way Sue cut tomatoes, a very fancy zigzag style. She gave him a demonstration of how she did it. Sue spent quite a long time chatting him up after breakfast—while I spent half an hour in the bathroom.

We drove the car to a garage and left it to have the tire checked. Then we walked down to the almshouse (built in 1512), in the chapel of which Father said a prayer. I didn't realize he was praying, and I interrupted his silence. We strolled over to the ruins of Glastonbury Abbey. Father was impressed by the tomb of King Arthur and Queen Guinevere. "Now, that's historical," he said.

I sat on a bench and watched the people strolling among the ruins while Father strolled around by himself for half an hour or so. Then I rejoined him and we went through the museum, which has a model reconstruction of the cathedral as it would have been before it was torn down and burnt by King Henry VIII in 1539, just after he had Bishop Whiting taken to the top of Glastonbury Tor and drawn and quartered, then the various parts of his body put in a barrel—and rolled down the hill.

We walked through the town. We went in a bank, and the teller, a snotty, spoiled-looking fellow in his thirties, obviously with managerial ambitions, asked for Dad's driver's licence when Dad was cashing a few traveller's cheques, so I said rather loudly: "Imagine, seventy-eight years old and they still ask him for his driver's licence." Everyone laughed except for the teller.

At the George Hotel, where Henry VIII had, according to legend, stayed and watched the destruction of Glastonbury Abbey from the window of his room on the second floor, we had a pot of tea, then went back to the garage, where we were told the tire was unrepairable. The "boss," a man named Russell, phoned Budget who said we would have to take the car to an ATS— Auxiliary Territorial Service—depot to have a new tire installed, free of charge. Russell was remarkably nice, and he refused to charge us anything for checking the tire and spending all that time on the phone. We drove off to Wells, without having visited Chalice Hill or Glastonbury Tor, and then to Cheddar (after which the cheese was named, of course).

After much driving through the extremely narrow streets, we finally found the ATS depot, where we had the tire replaced and the alignment adjusted. We were treated splendidly, and when they asked us if we had this kind of service in Canada, we had to say absolutely not, we'd never had such good service anywhere.

Then we drove to the M4 and over the Severn Bridge to Wales, where I took a picture of Dad pointing at the *Welcome to Wales* sign. We drove north to Tintern Abbey on the River Wye and had a cream tea at the Abbey Hotel. Dad loved the fresh cream, as Mrs. Carter had recommended it that morning, and piled it up like mountains on top of the jam on the toasted buns. I think he was supposed to put the jam on top of the cream, but who cares? We drove north to Monmouth, where Geoffrey of Monmouth came from, and also where King Henry V was born in 1387, then over to Llandridnod Wells, where we took a B&B for the night and spent an hour or two in the Llanark Inn, drinking HB ale.

We had a long chat, and at one point I said that we all want to outlive our parents—but no one wants to outlive his children. Dad said, "Run that by me again." I repeated it. He wanted to know who said it. I said I said it. He said, "That's a good saying."

While we were driving today, as always, Dad and I talked non-stop. We decided the narrow roads made him nervous, or at least my not-yet-perfect driving made him nervous. And so we decided to stay on the major highways as much as possible.

Also, when Dad sees something here that reminds him of home, he accuses the Brits of being copycats. But when he sees something here that doesn't remind him of home, he accuses the Brits of just wanting to be different. When I pointed out this dichotomy to him (in the friendliest way, of course), he just laughed and admitted I was right.

TUESDAY, JUNE 9

This morning at breakfast, Dad said he didn't like the cream tea last night. He said he wouldn't have it again. He did seem to like it at the time though, immensely. A week or so later he would forget that he didn't like it, and would have it again and again. Older folks are so cute!

We left our hostess, the elderly Mrs. Jones, and her husband, who had had a tracheotomy and could only speak in a whisper, poor fellow, and went down to the spa, which seemed fairly dismal compared with my memories of it from five years ago. We didn't go in. We drove a charming route down to Aberystwyth, where we parked and went into the train station. I wanted to check on ferries to Ireland and so on. We also talked to the gentleman who ran the narrow-gauge railroad up into the mountains—a twelve-mile trip at twelve miles per hour.

But we decided finally not to go. We wandered through the town, eating chocolate bars and visiting the tourist agency for sailing information. We were shocked at how expensive it was to take a car on a ferry, and we were later shocked to discover we would have to pay the car-rental agency a huge insurance premium if we were to take the car out of the United Kingdom.

We drove up to Aberdovey, where we ate in the Hungry Sailor and had a long chat with the Liverpudlian waitress, a boyish young lady with an accent thicker by far than Ringo Starr's, and very hard to understand. She had just returned from five months in California, where she had, among other things, worked in a Japanese restaurant in the Castro district of San Francisco. She said she loves Californians because they are so "peaceful"—but they used to get angry at her, especially when she called the Chinese "chinks" and the blacks "wogs" or sometimes even "fuzzie-wuzzies." Everywhere she went in the U.S.A., she said, people would listen to her unpleasantness and say: "Where the hell do you come from?"

We walked along the beach at Aberdovey at low tide, talking about the moon, gravity, and the four elemental forces, and marvelling at the huge stranded jellyfish patiently waiting on the beach for the tide to wash them back into the sea. Then we continued driving north, through a thunderstorm into the mountains. We reached Ffestiniog, but it was too late to take their little narrow-gauge railroad trip. We drove over a bar-

ren area surrounded by treeless mountain meadows and herds of sheep, and took a B&B in a seventeenth-century stone farmhouse near Bala. The owner, who had been born in the house, said that Abraham Lincoln's mother had also been born in this house, but a couple of hundred years earlier—which impressed Dad tremendously.

The house had been remodelled completely. Dad asked me to come over and take a look at the shower.

"Isn't this the most beautiful thing you've ever seen?" he said.

To me, it looked like a perfectly normal shower. I thought he might be speaking of the tiles, but no, they looked like perfectly normal tiles too. "I'm not sure I see what you're talking about," I said.

"I mean how clean it is," said Dad.

From our window, we had the most beautiful view of Bala Lake and the surrounding countryside.

WEDNESDAY, JUNE 10

At breakfast, our hostess gave me a wonderful old book of Welsh history to look at. But when I started reading it aloud, she quietly took it away from me. I guess she found my pronunciation of some of the Welsh names intolerable.

In the town of Bala, North Wales, I took snapshots in front of a pretty church. Dad took my picture in front of a row of houses with different colours of brickwork. He kept saying: "This is really different."

We drove to Ffestiniog and took the narrow-gauge tourist train down to Porthmadog. Some elderly women flirted salaciously with Dad.

"If there are no seats on the train, you can sit on my lap, dear," said one.

"Then he wouldn't be able to stand up," said another.

Then they started going on about the blacks and coloureds and Chinese and so on, and how they all have a chip on their shoulder—and why are they let into the country anyway? Like most European countries, Britain has its ugly xenophobic side.

In Porthmadog, we went for a walk, and went in for a pint, then took the train back to Ffestiniog. Then we took a drive up through the north-central part of Wales, to Llandudno. When we drove past Conwy Castle, Dad was impressed that the castle was so close to the town. He said he always thought castles were more remote. I said something about how in the Middle Ages towns would cluster as close to the castle as possible, for mutual protection, among other reasons.

In Llandudno, where in a fit of inspiration during a holiday visit, Lewis Carroll wrote *Alice in Wonderland*, we walked along the waterfront and all around town, went in a pub for a pint and played the one-armed bandits. Then we took a room in the Belvedere Hotel, right on the Irish Sea Promenade. I fetched some take-out fish and chips, which we ate with scotch mixed with Welsh spring water. We watched a BBC television documentary called *The Illegals*, all about Russian spies in the U.S. during the Cold War. The show involved a Russian spy who had assumed the identity and passport of a Canadian who had been supposedly killed in the Spanish Civil War. The spy entered the U.S. at New York and told the immigration agents he was only going to spend a few days in the U.S. before taking up permanent residence in Canada. I began to realize that Dad was losing his hearing—or maybe his powers of concentration—when he turned to me and remarked: "They never mention Canada on these shows, do they." I also began to see that Dad is a greater Canadian nationalist than I had hitherto realized. For instance, he was forever looking through the English papers for the tiniest reference to Canada, but always in vain.

THURSDAY, JUNE 11

We had a long chat with the lady at the Bendemere B&B on the Llandudno seafront. She complained bitterly about the obnoxious Americans who start singing "What are we waiting for?" when she's making the tea. And they, of course, would be closely akin to the ones who complain about how small the tomatoes are and brag about how big their tomatoes are back home. American tourists certainly have a bad name all over Europe. When people find out that Dad and I are Canadians, they usually say something like: "I thought you were too quiet and polite to be Americans."

At the old Roman city of Chester, we took a wonderful double-decker bus tour with much historic interest. Dad was amazed by the Roman ruins, the ancient amphitheatre, the old town walls, Tudor half-timbered houses still looking good after almost five hundred years, and a strong flavour of the Middle Ages.

He went in to have a little chat with the chemist about his hearing aid, and the chemist sent him to the optometrist, who told him the hearing aid hadn't been adjusted properly; when he gets home he should insist it be fixed again—and fixed correctly this time. This made Dad feel better, and he put the hearing aid away for the remainder of the trip.

We walked all the way around the top of the old town walls, with their gatehouses and so on. By this time Dad's feet were very sore, and I couldn't find the parking lot where we had parked the car. So I took Dad into the Cestrian Pub and sat him down and bought him a pint of beer, then went to find the car. The guy who ran the pub came with me, and we walked along the canal and finally found the car. He hopped in and directed me back to the pub.

Meanwhile, Dad had spent the whole time talking to the woman who ran the pub—the man's wife. When I got back, Dad got in the car, and I ran back in the pub and plunked a pound on the counter to thank them for all their help. They, of course, characteristically of the British, didn't want the money, but that was because probably they didn't want us to think that they had been so kind just on the chance they would get tipped. The man was originally from Liverpool, the woman from North Wales. The man worked as a mechanic, but business was slow, so he helped his wife in her management of the pub, where business was also slow. They had lived in Wales for a while, where the man, every chance he could get, would go into the mountains for fly fishing.

We drove along the M6 to Blackpool, where we played bingo, walked, devoured even more fish and chips, and Dad tripped on a curb which was where it shouldn't have been. He fell flat on his face and nar-

rowly escaped breaking something that shouldn't be broken. How he, at seventy-eight, escaped breaking his hip I'll never know. He was terribly embarrassed. It was worse for his ego than for anything else. I felt terrible because I should have been holding his arm. Another man picked him up and got him to his feet before I could get to him. Dad said that he had been looking up and didn't notice the curb. A woman passing by said: "This is Blackpool, don't look up."

Blackpool was full of Pakistanis in cars with interesting sayings, such as "Paki Power," and waving Pakistani flags—and there were hundreds of cops on horseback. Dad was very intrigued and finally went up to a couple of cops and asked them what was going on. Tension was in the air. The cops said it was the end of Ramadan and they were hoping there wouldn't be any trouble, but they were prepared for it if it came to that, as they put it so nicely. I didn't think there was going to be any trouble and we didn't hear anything on the news about it later.

We drove up to Windermere in the Lake District and took a fabulous B&B and talked to the lady, Chris, for hours, about all kinds of things. Dad was very talkative and excited about the trip. All in all, this has been a good day. Except for Dad's fall.

FRIDAY, JUNE 12

We took a crowded bus tour of the Lake District with the guide, Frank, his Yorkie Igor, two elderly ladies from Sussex, an elderly couple from Toronto—and two sexy sisters about thirty from Switzerland.

Frank was obnoxious and arrogant—a terrible combination. But there was nothing I could do. Everyone else was seeming to like him okay, and I didn't want to upset Dad or the others by saying anything. He started right in by telling us about all the places he'd been in the world, including all the mountain ranges he'd viewed. Then he started telling us that he had lived five years here, five years there, five years everywhere. He talked about all the "weirdos" (I think he meant gays) in San Francisco, where he had lived for five years. He also complained, and bitterly, about the Labour Party of England—with especially bitter words about Neil Kinnock.

Talk about kicking a man when he's down, as they say, for Neil Kinnock and his Labour Party had just a few weeks earlier lost a crucial general election—one they were expecting to win. This fellow simply talked about himself, in the most self-glorifying manner, for the whole six-hour trip. I don't think I was the only one who felt trapped. He complained about all the drunkards from Glasgow, the "low-life scum" from Liverpool, and what a "low-class" place Blackpool was. And that was only half of it. His whole manner seemed to be some product of the subtleties of the class system in England, and I felt that if I understood the system better, I would better understand Frank—not that I wanted to understand him, really. It was as if he was desperately trying to show the tourists that he was not "low class," and therefore, of course, showing that he was lower than low.

The trip wasn't completely a washout, but Frank was not the best guide in the world. In fact, he was terrible. He pointed to every town, river, lake, and mountain we passed, but that was it, which didn't help us at all. I would call out from the back, "What's it famous for?" or "How old is it?" or "What's it called?" etc. He would answer, but he had to be prompted for everything he said. Most often he would say, "I don't really know" or "None that I know of."

He told us that Dove Cottage, where the famous nineteenth-century English poet William Wordsworth lived, wasn't worth visiting because all it held was some old stick furniture. If we wanted to see old stick furniture, we could come to his place and see his stuff.

At one point, Dad and I went off by ourselves to Wordsworth's burial place, the churchyard of St. Oswald's, a wonderful old eleventh-century church, where we took pictures of each other in front of Wordsworth's tombstone. When we got back, Frank, who had stopped to let the people go shopping in the town, but who knew that Dad and I had gone to visit the church, didn't even ask us if we had enjoyed it. He resented the fact that we had gone there.

At another point, I said something about Wordsworth's church and he said: "It's not Wordsworth's church, the church has been there since long before Wordsworth's time." How can you reply to something like that without being rude? I just told him I'd been to school too.

The highlight of the trip, besides Wordsworth's tomb and the great natural beauty of the area, was the Castlerigg Stone Circle, with a square formation of irregular standing stones inside the circle. Dad was powerfully impressed. The capper was when we got back to Windermere. In spite of Dad's venerable age, Frank didn't even pretend to offer to take us to the B&B

where he had picked us up. The full amount was £38 and when I asked for Dad's senior-citizen discount he knocked off one pound. We didn't leave him a tip.

I must add that one theme of the trip involved the other tour operators in town, who, according to Frank, became very mean to him when he set up in business, going so far as to come around the middle of the night and scratch up his buses. Forgive my thoughts, but it occurred to me the scratching up of the buses might have been the work of disgruntled tourists who felt ripped off by taking Frank's tour. I should also add that I never figured out what he did for a living before retiring to Windermere and setting up the tour business. But it was clear that he wanted us to think he was a doctor. So at one point, when he was going on and on about his five years living in India, I asked him if it were in the medical field. He simply nodded affirmatively, not offering any further information.

At that point, I had the chilling feeling that he was a confidence man, some kind of congenital liar. And for the rest of the day I couldn't shake the feeling.

Dad and I went with the two sexy Swiss sisters and had drinks in the local pub. Dad enjoyed himself and had two pints. Verena was the younger and sexier. Kathrin was her older and more thoughtful sister. Verena was studying for the year at University College in London, and Kathrin was visiting her for a week. Verena was studying art history, specializing in art-deco architecture of the twenties and thirties. She suggested we check out the Mackintosh buildings when we got to Glasgow. Kathrin worked for the Swiss Bank, in the Peruvian department. Coincidentally, Verena was married to a Chinese-Peruvian who was a student of Spanish-language literature and was writing a book on the Peruvian novelist/politician Mario Vargas Llosa. Their other sister was studying Chinese, and their father was a retired architect.

They each kissed both of us on each cheek when we parted. Dad was terribly impressed and was convinced Verena had the hots for me. I hadn't noticed at all.

SATURDAY, JUNE 13

At breakfast Dad couldn't understand Chris when she said, "Do you want sausage?" She had flattened her vowels a touch so that it sounded like "D'ye wenne sessej?" So I shouted across the table at him, "Sausage." And then he got it, and tried to pronounce it the way she had.

At the other table was a guy who looked like an IRA terrorist just released from prison, or out on weekend leave. He had crude, self-imposed tattoos on his knuckles, his earlobes, his tongue, his eyelids. And he was wearing skin-tight jeans, Cuban heels, and a black leather jacket. And a lovely silver cross around his neck. His girlfriend had pink lipstick, hair dyed red, etc. When they were leaving, Dad abruptly said to him: "Where are you from?" I almost died.

"Pardon?" said the man.

"Where are you from?" Dad said, slowly.

"Originally?" said the man.

"Yes," said Dad.

"Ireland."

Dad looked a bit embarrassed and said, "Nice place," as if he'd visited Ireland now and then. "I thought I recognized your accent," he added.

"I hope so," said the man, with pride.

We finally took off and drove to Kendall, as the only Barclay Bank to be open on Saturdays was located there. I ran afoul of a motorist with high blood pressure when I tried to walk across the street to the bank. There was a traffic jam, and as I threaded my way through the stalled cars, one car pulled ahead just as I was about to step in front of him. I had a strong feeling he'd done it deliberately. The fellow was fuming. He rolled down his window and said: "For starters, you aren't supposed to park there, and you're not supposed to cross the street here." He looked like a former RAF officer. I gave him a big smile.

Scotland! We drove north on the motorway to Glasgow, where we had a guided bus tour of the city with a fellow named Angus. It was a much better tour than yesterday in the Lake District, and Dad loved it. There was a lot of history—social, military and criminal, as well as architectural—and it was all-around terrific. Dad and I had a pint of Tennant's lager in the Queen Street Britrail Station pub. I zipped into the John Smith's book-store and bought a copy of *Rob Roy*, by Sir Walter Scott. Traffic was manageable in Glasgow, amazing since it was a Saturday afternoon. We both liked the town.

Angus, the tour guide, told us he thought Dad's father wouldn't recognize Maryhill if he were alive today. Maryhill was the suburb of Glasgow where old George Brown McFadden had grown up before emigrating to Canada with his parents (and numerous other families) around 1890, even though he had been born in Brooklyn, New York, in 1875. Angus suggested we check out the Glasgow Room in the Research Library, and the people there would be pleased to help us find out about George Brown McFadden and his times. But it wouldn't be open till Monday.

So we drove north along the shore of Loch Lomond. Dad singing the song about "You take the high road and I'll take the low road." The beauty of the place gave him thousands of tiny thrills and chills. We stopped and he took some snaps, then we stopped again at an old seventeenth-century church that had been turned into a restaurant called the Black Sheep, run by a fellow named Gerald Black. We had dinner while listening to an Anne Murray tape playing over and over on the stereo. We stopped at a B&B on the road to Oban, £9 apiece, run by a little old lady with a flower garden. She

was running the place very nicely. A cloud of midges attacked us as we got out of the car. They were the first we'd experienced, but wouldn't be the last. They were so small you couldn't see them, but you could certainly feel them.

SUNDAY, JUNE 14

When we went to bed last night, it was pouring rain. It was still raining when we woke up this morning. Dad came into the room and earnestly recommended I not try to take a bath, or even a shower, because he did and after a full minute it was nothing but cold water.

We went down for breakfast early since we had said we would come down at eight-thirty, but by eight we could smell the bacon already. Mrs. Livingston had placed all the bacon, sausages, cooked tomatoes, and fried eggs in a big pot (the usual Britsh way), and placed it on a heater to await our arrival. The tea was steeping, with a tea cosy over it—in the shape of a big black ram.

Mrs. Livingstone was in the other room with her husband, who was definitely the strong silent type.

But the meal was terrific, even though she did not serve it, having taken steps, apparently, to avoid us as much as possible.

"She's respecting our privacy," said Dad.

"And her own as well," said I.

We drove through the rain to the town of Oban, then took a MacDougall's tour to the Isle of Mull. We thought the tour was going to include the historic island of Iona, where all the ancient kings of Scotland were buried and where the world-famous Iona Christian Community was located. But we were disappointed, especially me, since this was the second time I had visited Oban without seeing Iona.

But we had a good time on Mull, visiting the multicoloured town of Tobermory, and drinking Tobermory scotch in the village pub, and visiting the Guthrie Castle and Gardens, which Dad particularly enjoyed, especially when he found out that Sir Winston Churchill used to visit the place for occasional breaks during World War II.

We took pictures of each other at the castle. The driver told us the gardens were studded with "the finest marbles outside Italy"—but they turned out to be a series of whitewashed cement statues. At the end of the tour, I complained to the driver that we had been misinformed about Iona, but he didn't seem concerned. Back at Oban, we also complained to Bernie, the wom-

an who had sold us the tickets, but she also didn't seem concerned. Dad said she was a "phony" because I had broken my watch strap, and she pretended she fixed it even though Dad had already fixed it before she took it off him. She was about sixty and kept applying lipstick to her face whenever she thought we weren't looking, which adds to my feeling that Dad was right when he said she was a phony.

We drove up to Fort William and then east to scenic Mallaig. I think Scotland is more lovely from the road than from the train. From Fort William, Ben Nevis was stunning, but its peak was shrouded in mist, as it was the last time I'd failed to see it, five years ago. Dad wasn't bothered at all, even though the road was windy and hilly, and my driving wasn't as smooth as I wished it to be. What a rock that man is. I hope I'm as courageous as he when I'm seventy-eight.

And when we got to Mallaig, too bad, we were too late for the ferry to Skye. So we booked into the Anchorage B&B, and ate gammon rolls, and finished off our bottle of Glenfiddich. Dad decided to let me know what a fine driver I was, and how he's not at all nervous. What will tomorrow bring?

MONDAY, JUNE 15

We took the ferry over to Skye, driving through fantabulously heart-stopping mountain scenery, with the sun shining through low-lying clouds—all the way up to Portree. Dad shopped for a cap which I had promised to buy him for Father's Day, and we had lunch at the Portree Hotel. Dad seemed to enjoy Skye a lot, particularly the town of Portree. But he kept worrying about not being able to find a cap that fit, or rather a Harris tweed cap that fit, and he wouldn't settle for anything but Harris tweed.

We decided to drive to Carbost to visit the Talisker Distillery. But we somehow went to the wrong Carbost. There were two villages, both named Carbost, on the same island. When we finally realized our mistake and got to the Carbost we were looking for, rather than the Carbost we weren't looking for, the last tour of the distillery had already started. With hands clasped dramatically, I pleaded for us to be allowed to join the tour, and they let us in.

It was fun to watch Dad scamper up the three flights of narrow, steep, steel stairs to the room where the three giant vats were kept. He is using his cane almost all the time now. The tour was a success, but when it came time for the free samples, we were informed that they had been given out at the beginning of the tour. So I pleaded again, and again we were taken up to be given our samples.

We paid back all this kindness by buying two bottles of Talisker at £22 each in the distillery shop and sixteen picture postcards showing a beautiful aerial view of the distillery and surrounding area. The manager of the plant engaged us in a long conversation in the parking lot. He said scotch should be taken with room-temperature spring water, non-carbonated. Ice is no good because it freezes the oils, and it prevents the full taste from being released. We agreed that tap water is a no-no because of the chlorine, etc. And Perrier because of the fizz. And Dad was pleased because he never put ice in his rye.

The manager also talked about fishing and walking on the island, both of which he enjoyed. He introduced us to a new word, *spate*, meaning a river that is dependent upon rain. When it doesn't rain, the river dries up very quickly. And this had been happening a lot up to the time we arrived. They had just endured three weeks of temperatures in the high twenties—and with no rain.

We took the ferry to the Kyle of Lochalsh, on the mainland. Dad and I got locked in the public toilets there. Some smart aleck had removed the inside doorknob. I went in, then Dad followed, and he slammed the door. There was nothing we could use to pry the door open. I had visions of us spending the night in there, because no one would hear our shouts. The toilets were way out on the end of a pier. And it was so embarrassing.

But I climbed up on the sink and pried open the window. Nothing to be seen for quite a while, but finally two men came by and I asked them to open the door for us. They smiled and agreed, but didn't ask any questions. We got out, that's the main thing.

We started to work our way north along scenic roads, single track for the most part. We stayed at the lakeside town of Lochcarron. The woman who ran the B&B was from Liverpool. She said she had come to Lochcarron for a one-week holiday forty years ago and hadn't gone home yet. We had a view of the long narrow lake from our room.

TUESDAY, JUNE 16

Today we drove all the way up to John O'Groats, the northernmost town on the Scottish mainland. Here is a postcard I sent to my brother Jack (and others).

> Dear Jack (and others):
> Here we are in a small pub with a large pool table in John O'Groats on the northernmost tip of Scotland. Tomorrow we're taking a tour of Orkney. Day before yesterday we drove all around the Isle of Skye, and visited the Talisker Distillery. But get this, Dad is an excellent pool player. We played four games tonight, with everyone in the pub watching. I beat him handily the first two games. The third game he rallied, and after chasing the black ball around for five minutes he sunk it, to the cheers of everyone. The fourth game also went down to the black ball but I got it. How about that? Every word guaranteed true.

WEDNESDAY, JUNE 17

A wheezy, cigar-smoking tourist from Arizona did his best to spoil the Orkney trip for us. It was one disparaging remark after another.

"What's the Italian victory sign?" he said. This was when we were visiting an angelic little church built by Italian prisoners during World War II. Then he held his arms up in a surrender gesture. And on and on. As

we were entering Maes Howe, the prehistoric Orkney burial mound, much like Newgrange in Ireland but a bit smaller, he came out, saying, "It's good for nothing." Actually it was marvellous. It had been broken into in AD 1000 by Vikings, and there was a lot interesting Viking graffiti scratched in the interior walls, including a cryptic remark about where the Vikings had taken all the treasure they had found.

Our man from Arizona at one point grabbed the young lady guide at the stone-age village of Skara Brae and said, "Why did they bother burying the women? Women are no damn good," with a stupid leer on his face. I guess it's guys like this that give Americans a bad name.

But we had a beautiful tour of Orkney. Very cold, and no trees, but Dad loved the old World War II ships that had been sunk by sneaky German submarines. Some of the sunk ships you could still see sticking up above the waves. He was particularly amazed by one ship that had been sunk fifty years ago, and it was still sending up a thin stream of oil.

We also visited a stone circle on the main island, saw the house where the first civilian casualty of World

War II occurred (he was hit by a German bomb), and visited the sturdy old Norwegian cathedral of St. Magnus in Kirkwall.

THURSDAY, JUNE 18

We drove down from John O'Groats. It was slightly warmer today—sunny but still cool. A beautiful drive, stopping now and then to look through the binoculars at distant castles or cairns, or, in a couple of instances, immense modernistic twentieth-century hilltop sculptures. In Inverness we took a bus tour, which included the Culloden battlefield. It was a rather disappointing tour, for Dad anyway, because he couldn't hear the driver very well through the speakers, even after we came down from the top deck.

Shopping. Dad still hasn't been able to find a Harris tweed cap his size. He found a blended material that fit well today, and the price was right, but he said he wanted to hold out for a Harris tweed, because he likes the look of mine. I had suggested he get a Gillette Sensor razor, since I love mine so much, and there was an ad in the paper this morning that they were only £1.45 at Sainsbury's. Well, we found a Sainsbury's in the Inverness High Street and Dad went in. He came out fifteen minutes later empty-handed. Turned out the salesgirl had no idea what he was talking about. All they sold was women's clothing. It was Salisbury's, not Sainsbury's. My mistake. Sorry, Dad.

We also went in the Safeway, to get granola bars and prunes. Dad had been constipated, but I gave him a big dose of psyllium husks this morning and he is all right now.

We drove along Loch Ness without even a glimpse of the monster, and then down to Perth through the heart of the Highlands, including the town of Dalwhinnie, where there is a distillery that looks like a village of whitewashed houses. We stopped for petrol rather than scotch. This is the highest town in Scotland and the scenery was magnificent. We had a nice B&B in Auchterarder. The hostess's name was Mrs. Armour.

FRIDAY, JUNE 19

Mrs. Armour and I had a long chat while we were waiting for Dad to come down in the morning for breakfast. She said her daughter had married an American medical student at the University of Edinburgh, and after he graduated the couple moved to Washington, D.C., where he soon became head of all the emergency wards in the city's hospitals. He was also asked to take an administrative job in the California health department and he agreed, so he now had two full-time jobs and was always commuting between California and Washington.

In the meantime, Mrs. Armour's husband had a heart attack. His family physician was treating him, but he did not refer him to a specialist. When the son-in-law heard about this, he bloody well hit the roof. He phoned the general practioner and demanded to know why he hadn't referred the old boy to a specialist. The GP said it was because of his age; if he had been younger, say forty, he would have done so. This time the son-in-law really hit the roof. He said, "So you practice selective medicine in Britain now, do you?" He phoned someone he knew who was a cardiac specialist in an Edinburgh hospital and the old man started to go to him. "I think if he had stayed with his family doctor, he wouldn't have been alive today," said Mrs. Armour. "I think this new doctor saved his life."

The son-in-law returned to Scotland and went to see the facilities at the Edinburgh hospital. They were so out of date, he was shocked.

Okay! We drove down from Auchterarder to Edinburgh. I was very sleepy, as if I hadn't woken up yet, or as if Mrs. Armour's tea had no caffeine in it. I kept looking for a place to stop for a cup of strong coffee. Before

I knew it, we were sailing through the outer suburbs of Edinburgh and Dad was already sitting up straight in his seat and saying things like, "This is a beautiful city." When we got downtown we drove around and around, waiting for a parking spot to become available. All the parking ramps had electronic signs saying *FULL*. Finally we found one near the Spring Gardens, at the base of the castle.

Dad was brilliant as he climbed the steep stairs up to the castle, with many thanks for suggesting he bring his cane. He would never have thought of it, he kept saying, but also would not have been able to walk half so well without it. He didn't get tired as quickly as he ordinarily would without the cane.

At the gate of the Edinburgh Castle, we noticed the plaque commemorating the 340 witches who were burned at the stake at that point—between 1600 and 1800, or something like that. Actually, the plaque had been removed, and a new one installed, since my last visit five years before. Apparently, people were complaining, because of the gory details, of course. The new plaque just said many witches were burned at this site, without giving the number or the dates. Politics!

Along the Royal Mile, we stopped in a shop. Dad found what we had been looking for all our time in Scotland: a genuine Harris tweed cap, and in his size, large. It looked terrific on him. I caught the saleswoman checking him out adoringly, and so I whispered in her ear: "How would you like to adopt him?"

"I wouldn't mind," she said with a big smile. I told Dad later and he enjoyed the joke. And as for his hat, he loves it. He's forever looking at himself in mirrors, and shop windows. I think he's going to be wearing it all the time from now on. It does look very spiffy on him, and it's a perfect fit. He's glad he didn't settle for a "blended fabric" cap, or one that wasn't a perfect fit. It's ironic that it took us so long to find one, and in Scotland too. I told him it was my Father's Day gift for him.

I had a pint of Caledonian, and Dad had a half pint, in an old sixteenth-century pub on the Royal Mile, and I told Dad what Caledonia meant and why all the streets in the town of Caledonia, Ontario, were named after Scottish place names. He didn't know that Caledonia was the name ancient Romans called Scotland, and he was surprised that none of his Scottish friends, such as the late Tommy Hay and others, had ever mentioned this, especially when they lived so close to Caledonia, Ontario. He figured that maybe they didn't know either, even though they were born and bred in the land of the Scots.

Dad did a lot of walking, with his cane of course, and now, also, his spiffy new cap. When we got into the castle he was terribly impressed by the small room with fireplace in which Mary Queen of Scots had given birth to James VI of Scotland (also known as James I of England). It was preserved exactly as it was, except that the ceiling had been repainted when King James returned for a brief visit as a grown man. The date of his birth had been painted on the ceiling, very elaborately, in Latin. It was June 19, 1566. We chatted with a small friendly man about thirty-five, with a lot of historical knowledge, who worked at the castle as a guide. He asked if we knew the date today. I checked my watch. It was June 19. He said, yes, it's King James' birthday. We were very impressed. He said, yes, it's his 426th birthday today.

This of course is the King James I whose name is commemorated in the King James version of the Bible, the one that was published during his reign and in the forty-sixth year of Shakespeare's life. In fact, it is, to my mind, certain that Shakespeare was at least a part-time member of the translation team. Irrefutable proof is available upon request.

Later, when we went into the Great Hall, the same fellow showed up and walked over to us with a big smile.

Dad asked him about the little Georgian mortars that were on display, and he explained them in great detail, and how they worked. They would have been state of the art when most of present-day Edinburgh was being built.

Dad also loved the Scottish war memorial, which is housed in an old building in the Crown Square of the castle. It was very moving. The names of every man who fought in a British or Colonial outfit and was killed in the war were on display in a series of leather-bound books, regiment by regiment, battalion by battalion. We found a Charles McFadden of Glasgow who was killed in World War I. They also had books devoted to all the Scottish civilian casualties, and one or two for all the servicewoman casualties. There were some moving battle scenes in bronze. There was even a memorial to the animals that were killed. And a series of four stained-glass windows, one for each season, showing idealized scenes of childhood, and scenes from the war. At the central shrine is a silver casket containing the roll of honour of the 100,000 Scots who fell in World War I. Dad kept commenting on the futility of the war. Both of us had a hard time keeping the tears back.

As we climbed back down from the Castle and were almost back to our parking lot, a Guide Friday bus came by and stopped right where we were. We had been vaguely planning to head straight out of Edinburgh and down to the south, but when the bus pulled up, Dad said, "I guess it was meant to be," and we hopped aboard. The guide was a young fellow with a Canadian accent who bore a striking resemblance to my friend George Bowering. It turned out he had been born in Orkney and had gone to Canada as a child with his parents. He lived for eighteen years in Newfoundland and two years in Toronto. He had lived in the Bloor and Bathurst area in Toronto, right next to Honest Ed's, and had married an American woman living in Toronto. But the marriage turned sour, so he took the opportunity to move back to Scotland. He said much of his family were living in the Edinburgh area and he was very happy there. I told him I loved Edinburgh and would prefer it over London as a place to live, and he agreed enthusiastically. He wanted to know what I did, and I told him.

He then spoke of George Mackay Brown, the Orkney poet, and said that he knew him. He said Mackay had just celebrated his seventieth birthday. He said he was a terrible drunk who spent all his waking life drinking in the pubs of Stromness. I was surprised to hear it because *sober* would have been the first word I would have thought of to describe his writing. He agreed. He was about to tell me his theory of why this should be when he stopped and said that although he wrote poetry himself, he didn't feel up to discussing literary theory with me. He later said he was still doing Canadian studies on a part-time basis and would check out my work. I had the feeling he meant it. His name was David. I didn't get his last name.

So we finished the tour, got back in the car, and headed south. At the border, there was a standing stone twelve feet high, with ENGLAND neatly carved on one side and SCOTLAND on the other. I took two pictures of Dad, one of him standing on each side of it. Dad was very happy about that.

We kept driving south, talking about how, as I've heard it said, one spoonful of sugar can shut down your immune system for four hours. Dad was quiet for a while and then said he had a theory about that. When we eat sugar, all the bacteria in our body go for it and gorge themselves, he said. They get lazy and can't be bothered fighting any disease germs that enter the body, such as the HIV virus and so on. I thought it was a terrific theory and told him he was really onto something.

We took a B&B at the Greenhead Guest House at Carterway Heads, Edmundbyers, Northumberland.

The lady's name was Peggy Bates. This was a very quiet B&B, with TV and bath *en suite*—up a country lane from the highway, with nothing else around except dogs, horses, and birds.

We had gone up another country lane to another B&B earlier, and Dad got out to inquire. As he did, a light in the upper floor went out. Nobody answered the door. But all the time we were there, a man in the upper window looked out at us. When he saw us looking up at him, he disappeared out of view, but we could still see him peeking around the corner down at us.

SATURDAY, JUNE 20

At breakfast I asked Dad if he wanted to take a river cruise, something I had been thinking would be a nice thing to do, especially on such a lovely day, neither too hot nor too cold, and in such a beautiful part of England as where we were: Northumberland. I showed him a brochure. He read it carefully, but decided he didn't like the idea, perhaps because it wasn't a very good brochure—it made it seem that the cruise was all eating and drinking and for large groups of people. Besides, we'd already taken a boat cruise on Lake Windermere in the Lakes District. And we were, as it turned out, to take a little cruise on the Thames in London.

As we ate, beautiful exotic birds twittered and flitted about in the garden, which we had a close view of through the dining room window. At the next table there were a couple of tourists from Edinburgh on their way home from somewhere, and I heard them talking to Peggy Bates about how the kids today, they want everything, right away, they're not like we were, they don't know how to do without and accept their plight, and so on. I suppose he was looking for agreement from Mrs. Bates, that "children today are indeed like that," so that would comfort him and make him feel that it wasn't only his own children who were crass materialists.

I wanted to butt in and accuse them of gross slander. For instance, my children, and my father's children and grandchildren, weren't like that at all. And most young people I know are not like that. But I didn't.

The man was wearing a bright red shirt. I finally got talking to him, and I mentioned that England had changed a lot since my last visit, four years ago.

"In what way?" said the man.

"It's becoming more Americanized," I said.

I thought to myself, four or five years ago you'd never see a Brit wearing a bright red shirt, for instance. Anyone wearing a bright red shirt would immediately be thought of as an American tourist.

"The Brits have discovered Florida," I said.

"We've been to Florida twice," he said. "And I think Britain could use a bit more Americanization."

"Well, maybe a bit," I said, somewhat chastised. After all, he lived here and would be a better judge of these things than a mere tourist like me.

Dad checked the oil, which was a big job as we had to get out the auto manual to figure out how to raise the bonnet. But the oil was okay. Then Dad checked the tires, making sure they weren't all ruined by the "loose chippings" we had been driving over. Then we took off along some side roads, which Dad liked immensely. "Very restful," he said.

We stopped at Pow Hill and walked along a path to a "bird hide," which would be called a "bird blind" in Canada. We watched some ducks through the binoculars, and I wished I knew more about birds, and that I knew all their names. I vowed to take up birdwatching when I got back to Canada. Then we drove on a narrow road to Blanchland, a village full of houses made of stone, and went for a walk through the town. "This is a real stone-age village," said Dad. He was amazed that there was no filling station in town—just one cricket pitch with a chair left from the night before, one post office, and one convenience store. And dozens and dozens of late eighteenth-century houses made of stone and covered with roses.

There were footpaths leading here and there and along the river, and I suggested we take a little walk along one to the next village and back, which would have been three miles, but Dad wasn't so sure he felt up to it, so we took off in the car. We went past the appropriately named village of Wall to a spot where Hadrian's Wall appeared, then parked and walked through a field full of bleating sheep to take a look at the wall.

Dad wanted to know who Hadrian was. I told him the little I knew of the Roman occupation of Britain and how the power of the Roman Empire was waning and the Romans didn't want to have to endure further raids by the Picts from Scotland without reinforcements from Rome. And so the emperor, Hadrian, who couldn't afford to send reinforcements, and who had actually visited Britain, ordered that a wall be built from coast to coast to keep the Picts out—with inexpensive slave labour and local stone.

Then we cut over to the A68. Dad wanted to know what the "A" stood for. I didn't have a clue. He said the "I" in highways in the United States stands for Interstate, what the heck does the "A" stand for? I suggested maybe avenues. Avenues? he said. These aren't avenues, certainly, are they?

So I thought about it and decided that before the building of the motorways in the early sixties, the "A" roads were called that because they were the best highways in the country. And to avoid confusion, they called the motorways "M," followed by a number, and left the "A" road names intact.

So we finally got down to Clinton Moor, where you have the Park-and-Ride system for getting into the ancient city of York to cut down on the traffic congestion therein. There was also a nice little shopping mall at

Clinton Moor, and it looked like something from North Tonawanda, New York. So I asked Dad if he wanted to go browsing through the mall. I would go into the pub or a restaurant and get caught up on the travel journal. He thought that was a good idea.

So I had an hour to get caught up, and Dad wandered around and bought a Gillette Sensor razor for a special introductory offer of £1.45. This time he didn't have to worry about me sending him to a women's clothing store to buy a man's razor.

I sat in a large cafeteria-style restaurant and drank coffee that tasted not at all like coffee, but not totally bad, with parents with cart loads of groceries and screaming kids eating cream puffs at adjacent tables and casting glances at my typing away at my laptop. One guy I noticed glaring at me. Apparently my typing was interfering with his concentration. He was reading the *News of the World*.

Dad returned after about an hour and said he was disappointed in the mall. There wasn't much to see really, there wasn't even a central corridor, all the stores opening out only to the front parking lot, which was vast. He said the shopping mall, which was widely advertised as the greatest shopping mall in Britain, full of what the Brits called "superstores," was about on a par with the tiny insignificant Nash Road Mall in the east end of Hamilton, Ontario. We had a pot of tea, then took the bus into York.

We wandered around inside York Cathedral for a while, but I had the sense that Dad was tiring of cathedrals. So we took a bus tour of the city, and he much preferred that. The guide on the tour was a rather insincere young man with a penchant for snarky humour, alliteration, and terribly clever puns. But Dad found him suitably informative and seemed to get a lot out of the historical anecdotes and the views of the old walls and the castle and so on. Then we hopped back on the Park-and-Ride bus and got back to our car.

From there we took a long drive down to Doncaster, which seemed very gloomy and rather a tough town. It was Saturday night. All the young people were dressed up in their disco best and heading in the same direction, probably towards the local disco.

"Wow, look at that woman," I said as we passed a pair of high heels and a bulging skintight minidress.

Dad looked. "Would she be a prostitute?" he said.

"No, Dad. Probably not. Just a disco queen."

We headed east to Grimsby, an old fishing town that had seen better days, and though quite large seemed rather deserted. We bypassed Cleethorpes and headed towards Boston, searching for a B&B since it was getting late, but not finding one. Finally we stopped and asked a fellow if there were any B&Bs about. He directed us off the main road to a place called the Old Vine Inn or something like that. This was about twenty miles north of Boston. It turned out to be a pub with accommodation upstairs. Dad didn't like the idea of staying above a pub, for who knows what foul drunkard had stayed in the room the night before. But since it was so late, I went in. I was shown quite a respectable room by a very respectable-looking lady who complained of fatigue and said she had just been released from hospital after a surgical operation. I didn't request any details.

The idea of staying above a pub appealed to me, as I had done it before on many occasions without ill effect, and because one could go down and enjoy a pint and some pub chat before retiring. But I didn't want to rave to Dad about the room, and when I went out and told him it was okay, it was obvious he wanted to take a chance on finding something better down the road. So off we went. He said he would have gone in if I had told him it was wonderful and that he'd be sure to love it. But I didn't want to abuse his confidence in me. What if I had raved about it and he found something that displeased him, that I hadn't noticed?

By the time we were approaching Boston it was really getting quite late, but we finally found what seemed like a good B&B there, in an old Georgian stone house. It was run by an elderly lady who claimed to be seventy-nine. She asked for Dad's age and when I told her, she calculated that she was six months older than him, and so she took the opportunity to start telling all about her memories of World War I. So it seemed she had probably cut a few years off her age, for Dad certainly didn't have any memories of World War I. Then she said something about being eight years old at the end of the war, which was probably closer to the truth, and which made her eighty-two, to Dad's seventy-eight.

She told us some horrible stories about the German bombing of Grimsby, where she was from, stories that made quite an impression on Dad, including one story about three boys picking up an undetonated bomb which then detonated, and all that was found of the boys was a single solitary thumb. She was also rather xenophobic and still harboured a dislike of Germans as well as other racial groups. She said she wanted to go down to Dover and blow up the Chunnel. She also disliked the Japanese. She said she had a Japanese guest once and he kept writing things down in a book. She figured he must have been a spy for some Japanese corporation. I figured he was a simple poet, recording his impressions of England in his travel journal.

When Dad and I got in the room, we could hear a terrible buzzing sound but we couldn't figure out where it was coming from. At one point it seemed to be coming from the next room, then from under one of the beds, then from the street. It was very perplexing. We were getting nervous. I was all set to go down and ask our hostess to check it out, when Dad suddenly discovered the source. It was his suitcase. Apparently his razor, which had been carefully packed that morning, had somehow started up under its own steam.

SUNDAY, JUNE 21

There were some nice Americans at breakfast. There was a middle-aged man and his wife from Atlanta, who said they used to live in Michigan so they knew about Canada. Sitting on the sofa were their elderly mother and father. It was Sunday and everybody was preparing to go to church, but they were also looking up ancestral haunts. They had just arrived from the U.S.A. the day before and they were pleased to inform us that in the past couple of weeks the presidential campaign of

H. Ross Perot had peaked and seemed to be slipping considerably. They didn't like George Bush either, so Dad figured they must have been Clinton supporters. After poking around old churchyards in Norfolk, they were going to fly to the Netherlands to visit old friends.

"Fly? To the Netherlands?" I said.

"We know it's just a few miles across the water, but our friends insisted we fly because they're so anxious to see us."

After breakfast, the Americans flew off, and Dad had a longish talk with our hostess about the war while I browsed through her collection of old books on Norfolkshire. While Dad packed his bag, I wandered back behind the house and through a beautiful English-style garden and back to an old stone windmill dated 1812. When I got back, Dad was in the garden by the car and chatting with the woman's son, a huge friendly man who ran a pub down the street. They were talking about the Falklands War.

We hopped in the car and drove into Boston, where we got caught in a traffic jam. That gave us a good view of the little town, which had given its name to the much larger and more famous American city through its association with the Pilgrim Fathers, who came from this area. We spoke of the antiquity of England, and its respect for traditions. Dad kept saying that in Hamilton all these old buildings would have been long torn down, and replaced with shiny new buildings completely lacking in charm and character and which would be falling apart in a decade.

Soon we were out in the flat countryside of Norfolkshire, driving to the prosperous-looking twelfth-century town of King's Lynn, on the Great Ouse, which flows north a few miles into the Wash. It looked a lot like the Netherlands. We drove past Sandringham House, a neo-Elizabethan mansion belonging to the Queen, and the place where both Kings George V and

VI had died, and on up to Walsingham, where there is an old shrine dedicated to Our Lady of Walsingham. It commemorates a vision of the Virgin Mary which appeared to the lady of the manor in 1061. In the Middle Ages the shrine was famous all through Europe and attracted pilgrims, who enjoyed reporting cures.

It was Sunday morning. High mass was in progress. Organ music could be heard from the church. My former Toronto neighbour, Michael Coren, had asked me to bring him back a statue of Our Lady of Walsingham if I were in the area, and I felt as if I were on a sacred mission to do so. I was worried that the gift shop wouldn't be open, since it was Sunday, and sure enough it was closed. But a sign said it would open after mass. So we had a pot of tea and a sandwich in the little café there. Dad and I visited the two old shrines on the premises, one Catholic and one Church of England. It was all very peaceful.

When the gift shop opened, I went in and told the saleswoman what I wanted. She was very helpful. She got out all the statues of Our Lady of Walsingham, who was always pictured sitting on a throne and looking very early medieval, and with the infant Jesus in her arms.

"Choose which one you want," she said. "You'll notice they're all hand-painted and each one has a different look." I went through about twelve of them. They were all very attractive in slightly different ways, but I finally settled on one that I thought Michael would like. I also bought Michael a special plastic bottle marked "Holy Water from Walsingham" and filled it with water from the large spring-fed fountain nearby.

We hopped in the car and drove along the coastline, past little villages and beautiful old churches. We passed Wells-next-the-Sea, which Dad thought was just another example of the English trying to be different. They should have called it "Wells-by-the-Sea," he said, so that it would be like Lauderdale-by-the-Sea in Florida. I said maybe now that the English have discovered Florida they would change the name to Wells-by-the-Sea, to be more with-it.

We passed through Sheringham and Cromer. It was a warm Sunday and the beaches were full of weekenders from the city of Norwich and elsewhere.

At Cromer, we drove inland to Norwich, which looked like a ghost town. Everyone was at the beaches. We had the whole town to ourselves. We parked the car and walked around, crossing the various bridges over the Wensum River.

Norwich is filled with old bridges, churches, and a huge castle. We had a good look at the cathedral, but since Dad was understandably getting tired of cathedrals, we didn't go in. He kept saying I should go in by myself and he'd sit there on the bench, but I didn't feel like leaving him. I really found myself with no interest other than helping him enjoy himself as much as possible.

Ordinarily I would have wanted to spend all day in such a cathedral, but I wouldn't have enjoyed it at all today.

The afternoon sun was very hot, so we stopped off in a little café and had a Coke to cool off. It was about the only place in town open, and we were the only customers.

The man and woman running the place looked like brother and sister. I asked if they were. The man said with a smile: "Next best thing."

The woman said: "We're business partners."

Dad got a kick out of that, and repeated the story to several others in the days to come.

Meanwhile, back in the car, we drove down to London, which we reached at dusk. As soon as we got off the motorway, we got in trouble. London is an impossible city to drive in if one is not entirely familiar with it. Even with a good map, every little street is curved and twisted and, by golly, there are no rectangular blocks. Nothing seems to be properly signposted. But with the

help of a very kind East Indian filling-station opera-
tor who gave us explicit directions, we got down to the
central part of London.

We parked on Little Smith Street, which wasn't all
that little, and we walked around Westminster Abbey.
We also synchronized our watches with Big Ben, and
Dad got his first look at the Thames, the great river
he'd been hearing about all his life. His eyes were
shining. But, oddly enough, he kept thinking he was in
New York. "New York?" I'd say, and he'd say: "Oh, what
am I thinking of, I mean London. I don't know what's
the matter with me, I keep thinking I'm in New York."

On a previous trip to London, I had stayed at a B&B
in Hampstead run by Cathy Smith, an Englishwoman
who had run a restaurant in Vancouver for several years
and was a friend of my friend Margaret Hollingsworth.
But that was five years previous. I dialled Cathy's number from a booth near Westminster Abbey, not knowing if she still lived in Hampstead or if she still ran a
B&B. But she answered, and she said we could come
up straightaway. But we could only stay tonight since
she had a friend from Vancouver coming in the next
night for two weeks.

Night had fallen. We had a hard time finding Finchley Road, but with the help again of people in filling stations we finally made it to Cathy's place. She was very
helpful and Dad liked her immediately. She said she
had made a mistake, we could stay for two nights, her
friend wasn't coming in until Tuesday. We brought our
bags in and we got out our scotch, and all three of us
had a couple of drinks.

And then, after we had our drinks, she said what
the heck, we could say as long as we wanted, because
her friend from Vancouver could sleep in an extra bed
in her room. Furthermore, we could leave our car on
the street, there was no problem in parking. So we felt
very lucky.

MONDAY, JUNE 22

The next morning, after a wonderful breakfast of crepes suzettes ("How did you get these pancakes so thin?" said Dad) and tea and toast and marmalade, Dad and I went into the news agent's and bought a couple of Travelcards. These allowed us unlimited tube and bus travel around London. We took the bus to Trafalgar Square and wandered around. We went past the Churchill War Rooms, which interested both of us greatly, but we decided not to go in right away. We would wait till later. This of course was a mistake, since we never did get back to them.

We slipped over to Saint James Park, within sight of Buckingham Palace, and sat on a bench and watched the swarms of tourists marching to and fro. Dad, like me, is a great people watcher. We watched an old codger on the bridge feeding the little sparrows and chickadees. They were so tame they actually landed on his arm and ate out of his mouth.

But the lives of sparrows and chickadees are not always pleasant. As we walked towards the palace, we saw a horrible sight. A gull had caught a small blackbird and was viciously tearing it apart and stabbing it in the heart repeatedly with its beak. Dad was very upset at this. Neither of us had ever seen anything like it, all the worse for us because it was taking place in such peaceful and beautiful surroundings. Dad said the gull was probably retaliating because the poor blackbird had stolen some of its food.

We kept walking, around the massive Queen Victoria Memorial in front of Buckingham Palace, and then over to the palace itself. The Royals were not in residence, but I was able to point out the windows of the Queen's apartments, for Dad's pleasure.

Even though Dad was tired of cathedrals and old churches, he couldn't resist Westminster Abbey, because of its fame, and because so many of his friends who had visited London had raved about it. So we spent a couple of hours in the Abbey. It was packed with tourists of all nationalities, and a lot of intricate crowd control was being exercised by the staff. But we still enjoyed ourselves immensely. I had brushed up on my English history just before we came to England, fortunately, so I was able to fill Dad in on some of the historical contexts of the old kings and queens whose tombs and effigies we were looking at.

Dad was terribly interested in my sad story of King Charles I. He had been beheaded on a scaffold over the West Entrance of Westminster Abbey, in full view of a hundred thousand raving citizens who filled the old square to view such an historic and pivotal event that paved the way for the supremacy of Parliament and the relegation of Royalty to merely figurative status. Coincidentally, there were some repairs going on over the West Entrance as we stood there, and a scaffold had been erected in exactly the same place that Charles I's scaffold had been, 360 years earlier. Dad stared up at it in wonderment.

We entered by the West Entrance, and just inside there was a little memorial to Winston Churchill, a great favourite of Father's, and immediately behind it, surrounded by a splendid profusion of bright red poppies, was the Tomb of the Unknown Soldier. Dad had a hard time holding back the tears. It really is an emotional experience seeing that tomb the first time. I had cried and now Dad was all choked up. I thought I saw tears running down his cheek.

"I bet every parent who lost a son in that war feels that it's his body in there," he said.

We saw the Coronation Throne, on which every English monarch since William the Conqueror in 1066 had been crowned, including Queen Elizabeth II—and Queen Elizabeth I, for that matter. I told Dad all the stories I could think of about whatever monarch whose tomb we were looking at.

Dad particularly enjoyed the Poet's Corner. He sat down to rest and I said: "Dad, look what your feet are resting on." He looked, and it was a floor slab covering the tomb of Sir Laurence Olivier, who had died a couple of years ago. We also visited the circular twelfth-century Chapter House with its high stained-glass windows, and the eleventh-century Pyx Chamber, and the Norman Undercroft, with its ancient funeral effigies of famous monarchs. I bought a beautiful poster for my daughter Alison, showing Westminster Abbey as it might have appeared in 1527.

Later we took a little cruise along the Thames, from Westminster down to London Tower and back. There was a bar aboard and we drank beer as we sailed along. There were only three other people on the boat.

Dad has been saying all along that the Royal Family was a big drawing card for tourists to come to Britain. But on the boat he said: "The Queen and Prince Philip, they must think all these tourists come just for them."

The fellow on the loudspeaker was a bit of a bore. Dad found it hard to follow his cockney accent. He made a particularly hokey pitch for tips at the end of his spiel, saying the boat needed constant maintenance, as did his wife and their seven children. Dad gave him a pound, and I slipped three more for the poor fellow with so many kids.

Once off the boat, Dad took several pictures, mostly of Big Ben. At one point, a cab driver stuck in a traffic jam was watching Dad focus his camera on Big Ben and couldn't resist calling out: "Why don't you buy a picture postcard? It would be cheaper." Dad thought this was very rude, but I said he was just being friendly.

On the way home, we got into a bit of trouble on the buses. Dad had been unsteady as he climbed up to the top of the double-deckers while the bus was in motion, so we decided to stay on the lower deck. This time we had to go to Oxford Circus, then change to a number

13 bus up Finchley Road. So we asked the conductor to tell us when we got to Oxford Circus. He did, and with the bus stopped just for a split second at a roundabout, Dad hopped off. "Not now," called out the conductor, but it was too late. The bus started up again, forcing me to leap off while it was moving in order to join Dad.

Later, on another bus, a different style, the kind without the conductor and on which you have to pay the driver, Dad innocently walked past the driver without showing his Travelcard. The driver reached out and grabbed Dad's arm. Dad later told me he thought his cane had caught on something and he was trying to pull it loose. He lost his footing and almost fell in the aisle. I was livid.

"I don't think you're supposed to grab people," I said to the driver, sternly. He went on about how it was the law, and he had to resort to any means to ensure people paid. "You're lucky he didn't take a flyer," I said. The driver looked a bit chastised.

TUESDAY, JUNE 23

This is the first quiet day we've had since arriving on these shores. With Cathy Smith's permission, we lounged around all day, Dad writing postcards, me reading and listening to BBC Radio 4.

Around five o'clock, we went to the post office and mailed postcards to Bill and Helen, Jim and Marie, Alison and Mark—and we mailed Alison's poster in its mailing tube. Dad wanted to send more postcards, but he had left his address book at home. In certain cases he knew the address but not the postal code. I rang Canada House and asked if they could give me a couple of postal codes from the big postal-code book I was certain they would have. They said they couldn't do it, of course. I didn't think to ask if there was any mail for me there. I found out when I got home that there had been tons of it.

After leaving the post office, we got on a double-decker to Golders Green tube station, from which we wanted to take the tube to Hampstead for a walk and dinner. I told the conductor we were going to Golders Green. "Then it would probably be more appropriate," he said, "if you got off this bus, crossed the road, and took one going the other way."

Ouch. So much for my good sense of direction.

We finally got to Golders Green, went into the National Express office, and bought two round-trip tickets to Calais for £68. People there were very helpful. They bent the rules to let us keep our return date open at no extra charge, and they tried very hard, making several phone calls, to get the senior citizens' discount for Dad, but were unable in the end to do so because it was an out-of-the-country trip. Then we took the tube over to Hampstead. The train runs overground between Golders Green and Hampstead, but just before it reaches Hampstead it plunges down very deep—in fact, at this point it's the deepest station in the entire London Underground, and we had to take an elevator to get to the surface.

We had a pint in a pub in Hampstead and read a newspaper or two. A man was sitting on a barstool at the front window and he had a large English sheepdog. It was freshly washed and well-groomed. For some reason, the man kept staring at Dad and me all the time we were there, and not very pleasantly either. Every time we glanced up, he would be staring intently at us. Dad said when I left at one point to go to the newsagent's for the *Herald Tribune* to find out the latest baseball news (Toronto was still in first place), the man jumped up and watched me as I walked down the street; then, when I was out of sight, he sat back down and resumed staring at Dad. When we left, Dad said the guy was a "real weirdo," and he kept looking over his shoulder to see if he was following us. Dad said he wouldn't be surprised if the guy came out and started firing a gun at us. I said he couldn't have been that crazy because he had such a well-groomed dog, and so well-behaved. This made sense to me, but Dad wasn't convinced.

At an Italian restaurant in Hampstead, we had half a litre of red wine. Dad had lasagna and I had a pizza with capers and anchovies. It was huge, with English-style crispy thin crust, thicker than Italian style but much thinner than Canadian style. I said I'd only be able to eat half of it and I'd take the other half home for Cathy Smith and her friend from Vancouver, who was actually from Toronto as it turned out, Anna Buchan. But I ended up piggishly eating it all.

Anna Buchan works for a well-known architectural firm (the one that designed the Metro Library where my daughter Jennifer works). Anna is the communications director, which involves promotion and securing contracts and all that jazz. She needed a rest, so she came to London for two weeks, but she was also going to try to place an exhibit for her firm at an upcoming architectural show in London. She and Cathy talked to Dad quite a bit and had a host of suggestions for what we could do with our remaining time. Cathy talked about her eighty-eight-year-old uncle who lived in Yorkshire and who sometimes came down to London to visit her. She discussed the various places she takes him when he visits, and his various likes and dislikes and so on.

WEDNESDAY, JUNE 24

After breakfast, a mini-cab came to take us to Victoria bus station. The driver was a little Senegalese gentleman, and his equally little Vauxhall had leopard-skin upholstery covers. He was a quarter-hour late, and when we told him we had to catch a bus at eleven, he drove like a maniac, through very heavy traffic, and arrived with only two minutes to spare. After we paid him and he took off, I realized we had quite a long walk ahead of us, because he hadn't dropped us off at the right entrance. Dad was still a little slow on his feet, even with the cane, so I told him to keep walking and I ran ahead to try to flag the bus down.

There was a uniformed woman helping people board the bus. I told her my "poor old Dad" was coming along as fast as he could, but she said don't worry, the bus was running late and wouldn't be taking off for twenty minutes. So I relaxed and Dad caught up.

We stood in line with people waiting for the Cambridge bus at eleven-thirty. A French woman, who said she had been living in Melbourne, Australia, for sixteen years, allowed me to practice a little of my pathetic French on her (so to speak), and she complimented me on my excellent accent (the French are such flatterers) and said it would be very useful to have a bit of French on our trip, since there isn't much English spoken in the Picardy and Normandy areas. This turned out to be an understatement, of course. We were amazed when she told us she had just got off the plane after a non-stop twenty-six-hour flight from Melbourne. And that she was going to spend the afternoon at a meeting in Cambridge and then come back to Heathrow to take the plane tomorrow back to Melbourne. Dad said that must be a pretty important meeting. She said in her business (we didn't catch what it was) she had to do a lot of flying here and there around the world. In fact, she had been in Toronto last month. She was probably an academic with a rare specialty, such as the poetry of Andrew Marvell. Or maybe not.

A crazy old man with a styrofoam coffee cup in his hand approached us and started mumbling. He seemed to be trying to tell us the story of his life. I thought he wanted us to put money in the cup, but the cup had a lid on it so we couldn't. I'm not sure he realized it had a lid, he was so completely out of it. His shoes were tied on with rags.

"He won't be losing those shoes of his," said Dad.

When we finally boarded the bus, Dad got on first and took his seat, and I let a few people on before I got on. The same uniformed woman I'd spoken with earlier said in a loud voice, so that everyone on the bus could hear: "I thought you said your father was a poor old soul; he looks all right to me."

Dad heard that comment and was amused, but he was also embarrassed. Everyone started laughing. I called out to Dad that I had just been "exaggerating for effect," and everyone laughed even more. Then I said to the woman: "Geez, are you trying to get me in trouble or something?" The whole bus was breaking up. Dad saw the humour in it, and he took it well.

The traffic was still heavy, and it took us an hour at least to get through South London. The streets were full of people. I'd heard for years that South London was filthy, rundown, and "completely teeming" with blacks and East Indians. Well, this turned out to be another bit of British xenophobic propaganda, in the extreme. White people were clearly in the majority in South London. And it didn't seem as poor and rundown as I'd expected. In fact, considering we were in the middle of a severe recession and businesses were going bankrupt at record rates, it seemed downright prosperous.

Finally we got into the open countryside of Kent, the hills filled with yellow buttercups, red poppies, brilliant green grass, castles, and old churches here and there. It was a beautiful trip. At Canterbury, there was the famous old cathedral, the seat of the Archbishop of Canterbury, Primate of All England, built in the eleventh century on the ruins of St. Augustine's original church. I told Dad about Chaucer, whose tomb we'd seen in Westminster Abbey, and his *Canterbury Tales*, and also about the assassination of Thomas à Beckett (later sanctified) in 1170 and how remorseful the king, Henry II, was about it all, and about the miracle cures that were said to have taken place at the cathedral in the Middle Ages, after the assassination.

Dad loved Canterbury. The wide streets and clean houses made him think of Stoney Creek, or maybe Brampton. "I could live here," he said.

At Dover, we saw Dover Castle up on the hill, and the famous white cliffs. "I never thought I'd live to see the White Cliffs of Dover," said Dad. He started humming the song under his breath. We stopped at the downtown terminal, and a new driver came aboard, a young man about eighteen with a brand-new uniform. He had a slightly older man with him. The young fellow wasn't a very good driver, he had no confidence. He kept stalling the bus and was somewhat insecure in the roundabouts. When we got to the East Docks, he didn't tell us this was the end of the line, so everyone just sat there. The driver and his helper got out. We became very restless, didn't know what to do, so I went out and said: "Is this where we get off to get the ferry to Calais?"

He said yes, then got back on and said: "End of the line, everyone off."

I said to the helper: "Is this the driver's first day on the job?"

The helper said indeed it was.

So we all got off the bus and went to the departure lounge of the ferry terminal, but the door was barred because of construction. A fellow inside motioned us to go around to the back, which we did. But it turned out he was making a devilish joke—we were supposed to go around to the front. This struck me as very mean of the fellow, especially since there were quite a few elderly people with us, most of them carrying heavy bags, so I gave him a stern look as we went by the second time. Everyone was grumbling.

Finally, having found the main entrance, we went in. Dad and I had a beer in the lounge and I bought some papers and a pocket-size French-English dictionary. I told the bartender, a very kind and sympathetic middle-aged woman, that we were going to France to visit the Canadian cemeteries and battlefields so Dad could pay his respects to the brave Canadians who were maimed and killed. The woman seemed very moved by all this, and got quite choked up. She was close to tears and kept looking at Dad, who was sitting by himself, sipping his beer and reading the *Sun*.

"Oh, I hope it's not too sad for you," she said, "and you have a good time in spite of everything."

I rejoined Dad, and she still continued to give us sad looks, from a sad distance.

On the ferry, Dad took some pictures of the white cliffs of Dover. But he also took some pictures of the French coastline as it approached, and the skyline of Calais.

I was amazed at how many people spoke English in Calais. We took the bus into the downtown area and took a long walk to the train station. We were told there was no train to Vimy until tomorrow morning, and then we would have to take two trains to get there, with a ninety-minute layover between trains. I asked where the bus terminal was, and they didn't seem to know. So we hopped in a taxi and asked to go to the *"gare d'autobus."* The fellow took us back to the ferry terminal and charged us forty-five francs. I told him this was the ferry terminal, and we wanted to go to the bus terminal, but he said the bus terminal was here. All this in French. But it turned out there was no bus terminal at the ferry terminal, or indeed anywhere in Calais.

So Dad suggested we rent a car. This seemed pretty unusual, since we already had a perfectly good rental car parked on the street in Hampstead. But I went over to the Europcar stall and found we could rent a little Renault Clio for 640 francs (£64 pounds sterling, or $128 Canadian) for forty-eight hours, including all insurance and unlimited mileage. So I told Dad and he said let's do it. So we did.

I liked the little car. I also liked the French highways, and I liked driving again on the right-hand side. We drove along the coastal road to Dunkirk, but as we approached, there were factories everywhere belching horrible-smelling smoke into the air. The air was heavy, acrid with soot. Everything looked dirty. So we got out of there fast and took the road to Lille.

We had dinner in a little restaurant called Le Pomme d'Or. It was in a small village just off the road. We each had salmon with a glass of wine. The waitress seemed astonished that we didn't want a full-course meal.

We continued driving towards Lille, along the Belgian border. Dad wanted to go across the border just to say we'd been to Belgium. But I said we'd have to go through customs and change our money again, and it didn't seem worth it, and he agreed. When we got to Lille, we made a right-hand turn and headed southwest to Lens, where we found a nifty little hotel. It was called Ovax International.

Dad adored this hotel. Our room had twin beds, was sparkling clean, a good television, and *toilette en suite* with shower, etc. Dad was amazed, and particularly enjoyed the mini-bar and the hair blower—a good deal for 300 francs. The concierge spoke very little English, but we communicated well in French, until he asked me to park the car. For some reason, I didn't know the word for *park* and couldn't make out what he was saying at first. But we finally got the car parked, and the fellow came out and insisted on carrying our bags up to the room himself. When I told him we were going to Vimy first thing in the morning, he said: *"Ah, pour les soldats. Le monument canadien est très beau."*

In our room there was a very sexy late-night show on French TV. I told Dad not to look. I watched it for a while and could see Dad taking the occasional peek. It gradually got raunchier and raunchier, so I turned it off. In all innocence, Dad said: "I don't understand

how women could act like that in front of the camera."
I reminded him that in France bare breasts were no big
deal, just look at the beaches.

THURSDAY, JUNE 25
Another beautiful summer's day in France. We had a
café complet in the Ovax dining room, with *café au lait*
and little baguettes with butter and jam, and fresh fruit
and cheese. Dad was in heaven. Then we drove to the
little town of Vimy and up a winding, tree-lined road to
the Canadian monument at Vimy Ridge. It was spec-
tacular, and it made us very sorrowful, and very proud
as well. I had a rare old book at home issued to com-
memorate the unveiling of the monument in 1936, and
I told Dad I would give it to him when we got home.

We walked all around the monument and looked
down over the heavily industrialized part of France that
Germany had occupied during World War I in order to
provide steel and coal for the war effort. That was why
the defence of Vimy Ridge was so important. That was
why the Germans successfully fought off a French attack, killing thousands, and then a huge British attack.

But they couldn't fight off the Canadians. Four
and a half months prior to the Canadian assault on the
ridge, the Canadians began to arrive in the thousands.
The Germans knew they were there, but the Canadians
deceived them as far as their numbers were concerned.
The Germans had no idea there were thousands and
thousands of Canadian soldiers pouring into the area
and digging tunnels under their dirty noses.

While waiting at the tourist office for our guide to
take us through the tunnels and trenches, we chatted up
two young German soldiers in uniform. Dad thought
this was very ironic, and he took some pictures of us. I
rolled a cigarette for myself with one of the Germans' tobacco, and he rolled one for himself with mine—somewhat like the stories told about Vimy at Christmas 1916.

The tour guide was a young man from Ottawa. He was well-informed and had just the right tone. There were only six of us on the tour, including the two German soldiers and a middle-aged couple from Atlanta, Georgia. The couple had never heard of Vimy Ridge, but had just stumbled on it on their motor tour through France. They thought it would be worth a visit because they felt strongly about the fact that Canada was their next-door neighbour. I particularly liked it when the woman complimented me on the "intelligent" questions I put to the guide. She said my questions, and his answers, helped her to understand just what had gone on there.

Dad and I were weepy during the tour. It was hard not to be. Yet Dad couldn't resist his little jokes. At one point he asked the guide—just to relieve the tension, I suppose—if the soldiers had television in the tunnels. At another point, from the German front-line trench, I took a photo of Dad standing by the Canadian front-line trench, with his arms up in an attitude of surrender.

The guide told us the old stories about the Germans and Canadians exchanging little gifts at Christmas. And about a Canadian soldier sticking a loaf of bread on the end of his bayonet and holding it up for the Germans to see that they had a lot of food. The Germans retaliated by holding up a bayonet with *two* loaves of bread on it.

But it was incredible to imagine all these young men, the majority of them between sixteen and twenty—and one, according to the guide, only thirteen—all suffering in the thick deep mud and cold amid such death and destruction without becoming demoralized, and maintaining their courage and faith for the big attack. The guide spoke of how the Canadians decided to let off big bombs to make craters in the narrow no-man's land between the Canadian and German trenches, to make it less easy for the Germans to attack their position.

Now the craters, after all these years, are still there, but covered with rich green grass instead of mud. And the sandbags lining the trenches are still there as well, although they have been given a light coating of cement to make them more permanent. The boardwalks along the trenches and in the tunnels were cemented over as well so that the tourists, who started arriving from Canada immediately after the war was over, would have an easier time of it, and to prevent erosion.

Vimy Ridge was, as we were always told, the one big battle that had the most profound effect on Canada's sense of itself as a nation. For the first time, it became possible for Canadians to think of themselves as a country like other countries, rather than as a British colony. After all, the Canadians had triumphed where the British and the French had failed.

We went to the two Canadian cemeteries at Vimy and found ourselves alone there with the dead. The cemeteries are beautifully maintained, full of flowers, and acres and acres of perfectly cut green grass. A great sense of peace, and a great sense of war's futility, arose in both of us. Dad was particularly overwhelmed, and he kept choking up and letting loose the tears, and saying how horrible war was and what a great injustice it was that all these beautiful young kids had to die before they reached their full potential as human beings. I was as moved by the strength of Dad's emotion as I was at just being there.

So we went back to take another look at the monument. Some French stone masons were doing some repairs, and there was a lot of noise from a jackhammer, but it still seemed strangely silent—certainly much more silent than the ridge would have been at the time of the battle.

And off in the distance you could see giant slag heaps the size of Egyptian pyramids, and the many factories that had twice in this century been commandeered by the German armies to fuel the German war machine.

We finally left Vimy, and we drove along to Abbeville, where we stopped to walk through the beautiful town. Dad started humming "Roses of Picardy" and asked if the song had been written by a Frenchman. I figured it must have been written by a British soldier in World War I.

I popped into a leather-goods store, for I needed an extra couple of holes in my belt since I'd been losing weight since I bought it. The salesclerk thought I wanted a new belt, since I had taken it off and was pointing at it. But then I remembered the word for *hole* and said:

"*Un autre trou, s'il vous plait.*" And she said: "*Ah! Un autre trou!*"—and got out her punch and put two more holes in just the right spots.

Dad loved my story about Louis Armstrong, when he was travelling around the world giving concerts, and was becoming known as Ambassador Satch. Someone said to him: "How do you get along in all those countries when you don't speak any foreign languages?"

Louis said: "I is the pointingest cat you ever did see."

Dad, God bless him, thinks I speak fluent French; he doesn't realize how frustratingly poor it is. All he hears is me making unintelligible sounds, and other people making unintelligible sounds, and then whatever we want shows up, just like magic!

We visited a pharmacy to get some shaving cream. When I told the pharmacist we were from Canada, he got excited and got out a whole bagful of free samples for us to take on our way—little bottles of shampoo and bath salts and so on. French shaving cream and other toiletries are very good, and not very expensive. Too bad they're not more easily available in Canada.

Then on to Dieppe, a beautiful old fishing centre on the English Channel. It was dusk when we pulled in. We parked the car on the promenade. There were many holidayers on the beach at this point. We walked to where the cliffs began, and we went into a little seafood restaurant for dinner. We had a carafe of red wine and fillets of sole. It was excellent, but I was astounded that the waitress didn't know anything at all about the Dieppe Raid of 1942. Neither did the cook, nor the manager. At first I was astounded at what I took to be their ignorance. But later I began to realize that Dieppe was an ancient town, located in a strategic position, and over the centuries there had been many important battles fought there, both on land and out at sea. Sometimes what we take to be the ignorance of others turns out on closer inspection to be our own.

After we ate, we walked for a while along the beach. As it grew darker, Dad lagged behind, so I continued walking along. It was very hard to walk, with the stones rolling underfoot. And the cliffs were much higher than I had realized, much scarier, and it was obvious that they were impossible to scale, particularly by men loaded down with their rifles and ammunition, and without climbing shoes or ropes or anything like that. I'd read about Dieppe, but seeing it like that made me realize much more fully what a folly the attack was. How any Canadian soldiers survived at all, well, I couldn't figure out. How some of them managed to get to the top and were taken prisoner was hard to imagine. I felt that the soldiers who were ordered out of the landing boats and into water above their heads, as many were, and drowned, well, in a way they were the lucky ones.

By now it was so dark I couldn't see Dad, and he obviously couldn't see me so, I trudged back. I picked up a few good-size smooth white stones from the beach, pieces of chalk that had fallen from the cliff and been smoothed by the waves. And when I got back to him, I found out he had picked up a bagful himself. He said he was going to write on them, with his magic marker, "Dieppe: 1942-1992," and give them to a few select friends to put on their mantels. I told him that was a terrific idea.

We took a room in a hotel right on the seafront, with a beautiful view of the market area and the ferry terminal. It wasn't quite as spiffy as the Ovax Hotel last night, though. We pulled the twin beds apart by a few feet so that we wouldn't be snoring in each other's faces all night and were appalled to see the dirt on the carpet which had been hidden by the beds. I felt sorry for Dad, who is very fastidious when it comes to dirt, but he took it well, and both of us were soon fast asleep. No TV, so we couldn't watch any bare-naked ladies.

FRIDAY, JUNE 26

In the morning, we opened the blinds to see the Dieppe market. It was going full blast. Fishermen bringing in their fish, filleting them, scraping the barnacles off the mussels, and offering them for sale to shoppers, each of whom seemed to have a bag full of skinny baguettes about a yard long. ·

Dad didn't know that the French have such a fetish for fresh food. "No freezers in France, Dad," I said. "And no supermarkets. These people shop every day for the food they need for the day." He said it was amazing that people are pretty well the same all over the world, but they have such different customs.

Like many of his generation, Dad was a victim of the Depression—the Dirty Thirties. Because of the general poverty all around him, especially in a working-class steel town such as Hamilton, he felt compelled to leave school when he was only fifteen, even though he had high grades and has always been very intelligent. As soon as he left school, he took a job at the Steel Company of Canada. It was a demanding job, he claimed, but he was always wearing a nifty suit and tie, and he seldom got his hands dirty. Soon he was married with two kids. All his life he has never managed to find the time to read books or to take an interest in anything but the immediate problems at hand. That is why, in part, this trip is so important to him. That is why, for instance, he didn't know what had happened in 1066, he didn't know that towns were so close to castles, he didn't know the French like their food fresh out of the oven or the sea. And so on.

He was also amazed to see how friends greet each other so casually in France, with a kiss on each cheek, except for when two men meet—then it's a very formal handshake. When I was in the bathroom, he said, he saw a group of about six local gendarmes come up to the market stalls and very formally shake hands with everyone, shoppers and stall-keepers alike. And when two people meet who really like each other, such as a man and a woman, or two women, then they kiss each other twice on each cheek. And it's very natural, and it's without any self-consciousness.

We paid our bill. We were glad to get out of such a dirty hotel, in spite of the fact that it had such a splendid view. We had *café complet* in another hotel dining room down the street, actually a sidewalk café at which Oscar Wilde is supposed to have written "The Battle of Reading Gaol." It was fun to watch a fellow come up with a huge fish in his arm, still flipping, then stamp twice on the ground. Immediately a trap door opened and the fellow let the fish drop down—then turned and walked away.

"Why don't you walk over there and stamp twice on the ground and see what happens?" I said. But Dad said he couldn't do that—he didn't have a fish in his arms.

We walked over to the market and watched all the activity up close. We went into the tourist office and picked up a batch of booklets about the Dieppe Raid and a map of the town. We walked along the promenade, and I took a picture of Dad standing in front of

a plaque commemorating the deaths of something like 240 officers and men from the Royal Hamilton Light Infantry. Canada Square was a little park, with Canadian flags fluttering in the breeze and with a perennial floral display outlining a giant maple leaf. Also there was a large monument commemorating all the people from Dieppe who went to Canada in the early years, and also commemorating visits to Dieppe from various Canadian prime ministers, including Brian Mulroney just two months earlier.

High above Canada Square was the Dieppe Museum, in a huge fifteenth-century French château sitting atop the cliffs. This castle was German headquarters during the war. Dad climbed halfway up, but the steps were too steep for him, so he went back down, and I continued on alone. The museum was full of artifacts and paintings illustrating the history of Dieppe, but there was nothing about the Raid, so when I got back down and told Dad what I'd seen and what he hadn't seen, he didn't seem disappointed at having missed it.

Then we walked all around the town, stopping here and there for a beer or an ice cream or a pastry. We visited the thirteenth-century cathedral, Saint Jacques. And in the Park Jehan Ango, we looked at a sculpture by a Canadian named Michael Zarewko called *"Dieppe Alors et Maintenant"* (Dieppe Then and Now). It had been unveiled on the fortieth anniversary of the Battle of Dieppe, August 30, 1982, by the mayor of Dieppe and the Canadian Ambassador to France, Michel Dupuis.

The sculpture stands, in the form of a slab of concrete with a rectangular door in it and a steel, two-dimensional, life-size black metal silhouette of a man on one side of the door and another identical rough cutout silhouette on the other side. The first figure, apparently, represents the soldiers of Dieppe, and the other represents the soldiers of the future. Let's hope there aren't any more.

We hopped in the car and left Dieppe, heading down the coastal highway and through Abbeville, where we had been yesterday, then north through rolling countryside with lovely ancient villages filled with flowers, churches, and old stone cottages. We passed through Crécy-en-Ponthieu and visited the famous battlefield where, on August 26, 1346, an English army under King Edward III (his effigy at Westminster Abbey shows a sad-faced man with a long straight beard like an old hermit) routed the forces of King Philip VI of France. The French army had been pursuing the

English for a week, after the English had marched un-impeded through lower Normandy, destroying town after town, on the pretext that the French wouldn't recognize the English legal right to rule France.

A wooden tower on a hill commemorated the spot where a windmill had stood at the time. This was the windmill from which Edward III had observed the battle. He had about 14,000 soldiers with him, 4,000 riflemen, and 10,000 archers. There were three divisions, one of which was under the charge of the Black Prince, the eldest of Edward III's seven sons and the father of the ill-fated King Richard II.

The French army greatly outnumbered the English, but the English had the better position. Philip soon lost control of his men, and a series of unorganized assaults on the English defensive position ensued. About 1,500 French knights were killed, and thousands of other men, while the English losses were slight. This was just one battle in the Hundred Years' War. The slopes where the carnage took place are now under cultivation. Dad and I were the only ones there, except for a young woman sitting on the grass with her little boy.

I didn't realize it at the time but we were also very close, just three miles away, to Agincourt, the site of a more-famous English victory on October 25, 1415. This was the battle made famous by Shakespeare in his play *Henry V*, where Henry calls to his men, so sadly: "Once more unto the breach, dear friends." In this one, too, the English defeated a French army which greatly outnumbered them. The French losses amounted to something like 10,000, while, according to some chroniclers, the English lost only fourteen men. If I'd known we were so close, we could have visited that battlefield too.

We passed Boulogne, a beautiful city on the coast surrounded by medieval fortifications, still perfectly intact. We were anxious to get back to Calais that night, so we couldn't stop, but some other time it would definitely be worth a visit.

By late afternoon we were back in Calais. We were so close to Paris we thought seriously about staying overnight, then taking a quick trip into Paris the next day—"just to say we'd seen it," as Dad put it. But I was exhausted and didn't feel up to it. So we returned the car and hopped on the ferry, the *Pride of Kent*, full of noisy English schoolkids returning from a trip to France.

At the British customs, I got a bit snappish. I had gone to the washroom and by the time I caught up with Dad he was being verbally abused by a young customs agent. She was rolling her eyes and sighing because he didn't understand exactly what was required of him. She said she wanted him to fill out some forms and he had to do it right away.

I walked up and said I had the forms already filled out, then turned to two other customs agents who were standing idly by and said: "Where does she get off speaking so rudely to a seventy-eight-year-old?" They seemed to agree that this particular young woman was a nasty bit of business. At any rate, I didn't get into any trouble with my rather ill-considered remark, given the circumstances.

We were safely ensconced in a bed and breakfast in Dover by seven o'clock. We went down to the neighborhood pub for a pint and some fish and chips. This pub was named after the first man to swim the English Channel. But I forget his name. Paddy Webb or something like that. Then we went back to the B&B, had a good drink each from the bottle of Laphraoig I'd bought in the duty-free shop aboard the ferry, and fell asleep.

Now I remember—it was Captain Matthew Webb, not Paddy Webb, who was the first recorded person to swim the English Channel without the use of artificial aids, as they say. On August 24, 1875, the captain dove off the Admiralty Pier at Dover and swam for twenty-one hours and forty-five minutes, before he landed near Calais. The channel was forty miles across.

SATURDAY, JUNE 27

We were at the Dover terminal by ten o'clock to take the bus to London, but the driver wouldn't let us on because we had an open ticket, and the bus was almost full, and she had to give priority to those with a dated ticket. I said it wasn't fair, and the driver said: "Believe me, I know my job, I've been driving these buses for six years."

The driver's arms were covered with tattoos. Dad wanted to know if it was a man or a woman. I said it was a woman, because she had a badge on her belt saying: "The best man for the job is a woman."

So we had to wait for the next bus an hour later. We took a little bus ride around to see the sights of Dover, then got back just in time.

When we arrived in London, we went on a long walk through the Westminster area, then down to the Tate Gallery. We saw a display of Turners, also some Constables, Whistlers, Hogarths, and lots of other great paintings: Blakes, Picassos, Matisses, and a Degas or three. But Dad was too tired to enjoy them. His feet were bothering him. My feet always get sore in galleries too. He sat down to rest on a bench while I walked around to look at the pre-Raphaelites, and when I returned, his head was drooping in an alarmingly dejected position. He looked like a man terribly depressed, perhaps even contemplating suicide. When I told him so, he laughed and said no, he was just tired.

We had tea in a little restaurant nearby, and a man with a backpack and a Canadian accent, who had been sitting alone at a nearby table, said he had overheard us mentioning Canada and could he join us, as he was from Canada. We chatted for an hour. He was a Jesuit brother who worked with underprivileged children in St. John's, Newfoundland. We whispered about the

Mount Cashel Orphanage scandal, as well as many other things. Dad was very interested. The fellow had been visiting Ireland and was now about to head home. He left, then Dad and I finished eating, went to the washroom, and when we left he was standing outside on the sidewalk, waiting for us. Turned out he wanted to give us his card, and he did, saying if we were ever in St. John's to look him up.

We had a big Italian meal in the Spaghetti House in the West End theatre district, with a whole litre of red wine, most of which I drank. Dad enjoyed his spaghetti immensely, and I had pizza again. The English, strangely enough, seem to make the best pizza in the world.

We went back to Cathy Smith's place and thanked her profusely for letting us leave our large bags there while we took our small bags over to France. We weren't sure what we were going to do the next day. We didn't know whether to spend our remaining time in London or get out into the country some more. So we decided to go to bed and sleep on it.

SUNDAY, JUNE 28

In the morning, we decided to head out. London was too much walking and too tiring. I told Dad he could sit in the car and relax completely while we drove around to some of the beauty spots in the south of England. He was pleased. We had breakfast, settled up with Cathy, and said farewell, till the next time.

As soon as we got in the car, we knew we were doing the right thing. We drove along the motorway till we were well out of the city, then got on the winding A40 all the way to Oxford, which we drove around, looking at the ancient colleges and churches.

We drove up to Stratford-upon-Avon. We went to Trinity Church, at the altar of which Shakespeare is buried. It was Sunday and the church was in service, so we couldn't go in. So we walked along the Avon, Dad took two pictures of me with Shakespeare's church in the background and some swans in the river, and we took the little passenger ferry across. A performance of *The Winter's Tale* was just about to begin, and seats were available. But Dad figured it would be best to get a B&B, for we didn't want to take a chance on leaving it till after the play, and of course he was right. We passed a restaurant that advertised cream tea, and Dad wanted to go in, but I just wanted greasy fish and chips and a pint. So Dad went in alone for his cream tea, and I went down to the pub and had my fish and chips. We rendezvoused an hour later, and Dad said that that was the first time in his life he had ever eaten in a restaurant alone.

We found a B&B in a little side street near the church, but Dad decided he didn't like it. I went along with him, though I admit I felt a little miffed. It seemed okay to me. But his instincts were correct, for we went out of town and really got lucky. We found a beautiful place, a large suite of rooms all to ourselves, a living room with a good library of books, and a large colour TV, kitchen, large bathroom, and two bedrooms. All for the same price as an ordinary B&B. We watched movies till quite late, then watched an old Dean Martin/Jerry Lewis flick in the morning. It was called *Scared Stiff* (1953) and it wasn't half bad.

MONDAY, JUNE 29

After breakfast, we went back into Stratford and visited the church. Dad really liked the altar, with Shakespeare's tomb and the painted plaster bust of him and the famous epitaph:

> *Good friend for Jesus' sake forebear*
> *To dig the dust enclosed here.*
> *Blessed be the man that spares these stones*
> *And cursed be he who moves my bones.*

Some say it's a fake, Shakespeare could never have written such doggerel, but to me it's one of the great epitaphs of all time and could only have been written by the Bard.

On the way out, we met another father-and-son tourist team. They were from Japan. The son was about thirty and the father about sixty. The father had both his arms in casts. Of course, I asked what happened. He just groaned and shook his head. The son said they had been in a motor accident their first day in England. But they were bravely continuing the tour. The son asked me if this was a Church of England church. I said it was.

And so we said goodbye to Stratford-upon-Avon and went on a lovely little circular tour of the countryside around it, one selected from the large book I'd lugged along from Canada, *250 Tours of Britain*, put out by the American Automobile Association. I'd bought it in a second-hand store on Yonge Street for twenty bucks just before leaving. The tour took about two hours, with Dad navigating beautifully, the book on his lap. We saw a lot of beautiful little villages that would not have changed much since Shakespeare's day, and he probably had visited them all in his day.

We continued on our tour of the Cotswold Hills, heading up to Warwick, where we stopped for a brief look at the famous old castle, which bills itself as the "best medieval castle in England." And up to Cheltenham, where my friend Mark Howell comes from. And then we hit the M5 and zoomed down to Bristol, then along the M4 till we hit the road to Bath. We drove around Bath slowly, letting Dad see the sights, but without getting out and walking around. Same as in Oxford.

We drove south through Somersetshire, probably my favourite part of England, to Shepton Mallet, where old John Pidgeon, my maternal grandfather, had lived while attending the Blue School in Wells. We drove the road from Shepton Mallet to Wells, the same road that John Pidgeon would have taken during the years 1899 to 1901. In Wells we found the old school, though it's now no longer used as a school but as a little theatre and opera house. We took pictures of each other in front of the place.

We walked all around Wells, probably one of the most beautiful larger towns in England. We visited the Bishop's Palace with its moat which is usually filled with swans, all of which have been trained to press a bell for food. But the swans were on holidays. Lots of ducks, but not a swan in sight. And we took some pictures of Wells Cathedral, famous for having survived the disastrous reign of Henry VIII intact. But we didn't go in. Whenever we go in a cathedral, Father gets very tired, very quickly. I think it's because there's just so much to see and it's so hard to understand the incredible historical richness of everything there is to look at. So we got in the car and went down to Glastonbury and surprised Nick and Sue for a return visit.

Dad rang the bell alone while I sat in the car, and Sue Carter answered and recognized him straightaway. And the same room was vacant. We were in luck.

Dad wrote a postcard or two, and had a drink of Laphraoig, while I took off and climbed Glastonbury Tor once again. This was the third time I've done it, and each time it's been a sweetly mournful experience. There were some mean-looking hippies up there, ostentatiously meditating and chanting, playing flutes and gongs, but they didn't bother me and I didn't bother them. I'd never been up there when the weather was so nice. Warm and gentle breezes. And of course the splendid view of Somerset in all directions. I timed the climb. It took me exactly thirty-five minutes to get from the Carters' to the top of the Tor, and exactly thirty-five minutes to get back. Along with thirty-five minutes on top.

When I got back, Sue gave me a couple of old

books on Somerset to read, and I read them until about two in the morning, while Dad snored quietly in the next bed.

In the morning, Sue served breakfast as before and played Clannad on her stereo. I took Dad out in the backyard and insisted he sit there for half an hour absorbing the beautiful views out over the Somerset plain. The garden was full of flowers, and the whole countryside was so peaceful. "I just want you to sit here for thirty minutes, and say goodbye to beautiful old England," I said. And Dad said he'd be glad to. I left him alone.

The next time I come to England, I'll head straight to Glastonbury and stay for a week or two at the Carters'. It would make a great base for taking long walks through the Somerset countryside. I mentioned it to her and she suggested I come in October. "It's cool, there are no tourists, and the countryside is lovely," she said, and she'd pack a lunch for me on my rambles. I should also mention that she and her husband have a small indoor swimming pool and a huge pool table, both of which just might be available for the use of guests if they asked nicely, especially guests who were staying a week or more.

So we said goodbye to the Carters, signed the book once more, and drove over to Chalice Hill, one of the most peaceful places in the world. We sat drinking the spring water, and I gave the book to Dad to read, all about the many legends associating this spot with Joseph of Arimathea and, of course, Jesus. According to legends, Joseph of Arimathea had brought Jesus to Glastonbury to study with the Druids as a child, before he began his ministry. And Joseph of Arimathea brought the chalice full of Christ's blood to Glastonbury after the crucifixion and buried it on this spot. William Blake refers to these legends in his poem "Jerusalem":

And did those feet in ancient time
Walk upon England's mountains green?
And was the holy Lamb of God
On England's pleasant pastures seen?

And did the Countenance Divine
Shine forth upon our clouded hills?
And was Jerusalem builded here
Among these dark Satanic Mills?

Bring me my Bow of burning gold:
Bring me my Arrows of desire:
Bring me my Spear: O clouds unfold!
Bring me my Chariot of fire.

I will not cease from Mental Fight,
Nor shall my Sword sleep in my hand
Till we have built Jerusalem
In England's green & pleasant Land.

We spent more than an hour at Chalice Hill, and both of us left feeling refreshed in spirit and ready to say goodbye to England.

But not before another beautiful ride through the countryside, with stops at Stonehenge and Avebury. Dad never seems to tire of the old stones. "So here I am at Stonehenge," he said. He wanted to know everything I knew about it, which wasn't much. But then again, even the experts don't know that much about it really. And then up to the standing stones of Avebury, which in a way are said to be much more mysterious than Stonehenge, and vaster in scope and older. Dad found Avebury far more interesting than Stonehenge. We walked from stone to stone, discussing the shape of each one in turn, and speculating on what the people who had built this great prehistoric monument over 5,000 years ago must have been like.

Dad always seems to be at his best when we visit these great relics from remote antiquity. A certain look comes into his eyes. I guess we all love a mystery. He also liked the nearby Silbury Hill, a cylindrical pyramid of limestone and earth fifty feet high and 130 feet in diameter. It looks like a natural hill, but it was really erected by our ancestors, at roughly the same time as the stones of Avebury were put up. And nobody has a clue why this artificial hill was built, except that it had something to do with the Avebury stones since it was built at the same time and is within view of them. Apparently, scientists have used all the latest equipment on the hill and have found no sign of any ancient kings having been buried there, or in fact anything inside the hill at all. It was just built, for no reason that anyone can determine. Not even for any astrological or ritualistic or religious purposes. A complete and utter mystery. Something to think about late at night when you can't sleep. Maybe it was simply a place you could climb up to view the surrounding countryside, to view the Avebury stones and all the other prehistoric monuments in the immediate area. But then again, there are natural hills here and there, and they would have served the same purpose.

When we left Avebury, it was starting to rain, and so we headed east towards Heathrow, where we had a plane to catch tomorrow. Then the rain started pouring, so heavy that we almost had to pull off the road. We drove through the town of Hungerford, and I reminded Dad of the Hungerford Murders, a year or so ago, where someone went nuts and shot some people to death, then killed himself. And for the next few weeks, the streets of the town were filled with slow-moving cars from all over England, cars full of people who wanted to see where the killings had taken place.

"People have very morbid curiosities," Dad said. He remembered people heading over to Carrick Avenue in Hamilton, Ontario, to see the house where Evelyn Dick lived, after the dismembered torso of her husband was found on the side of the Niagara Escarpment in the late forties.

We wanted to get a B&B fairly close to Heathrow so we wouldn't have any trouble getting the car back in the morning and getting to the airport in time for our one o'clock flight. Then Dad had a brilliant idea. "Let's take a dry run tonight," he said. So we got on the M4 and drove along it until we got to the M25, then drove south till we got to Heathrow, and drove in till we got to the Budget Rent-a-Car office. That done, we headed back out with a stronger sense of security, and finally found a B&B in Maidenhead, after a long search.

TUESDAY, JUNE 30

In the morning, we drove straight through to the Budget office at Heathrow, handed in our papers, and took the little Budget bus over to Terminal 3 for our flight home. In the duty-free shop we bought some Balkan Sobranie pipe tobacco for Jack, as requested, but didn't buy any scotch, as planned, because there were no bargains this time. The Laphraoig, for instance, cost £20.99 for a litre bottle and £22.99 for a 1.14 litre bottle. We had seen it cheaper in stores in Britain. And, although I may have been wrong, it seemed to me it was cheaper in LCBO stores at home.

So we got on the plane and had a pleasant flight home, with splendid views of the west coast of Ireland and of the lakes of Northern Quebec. It was Canada Day, and we celebrated so much with all the free booze that was being handed out that we soon fell asleep.

During the flight, Dad told me that he liked me even more now that we had taken this trip together, and I told him the same. It also pleased me when he said that next year maybe we should fly straight to Dublin and do a little two-week tour of Ireland. This was all the proof I needed that the trip had been a success.

When we arrived at Pearson, my daughter Jennifer and brother Jack were waiting for us with excited looks. We hopped in Jack's new BMW, which was a big surprise, and a very pleasant one, and took Jennifer to the Kipling subway station, then headed to Hamilton to drop off Dad. Then Jack brought me home to Toronto, and even carried my bags up the five flights to my apartment.

I felt elated that the trip had gone so well, that Dad had seen everything he wanted to see, that he had enjoyed it so much, and so on. I had quoted Baudelaire to him at one point: "The greatest accomplishment a person can accomplish is to accomplish exactly what he has set out to accomplish."

Dad liked that, and agreed that we had accomplished something worthwhile.

POSTSCRIPT

That was twenty years ago. Dad is now ninety-nine years old. He is still living in the apartment he lived in with Mother, in the east end of Hamilton. When Merlin and I go to visit him, as we do every Saturday (or sometimes Sunday), we can see the actual spot where Mother slipped and fell from a chair when she was reaching for something on a high shelf. I think it was the right side of her head that did all the damage. She lived for ten years, but she was definitely losing her faculties. I was living in Vancouver at the time, but whenever I phoned home, Dad told me everything was okay. He didn't want to tell me what had happened.

But I sensed something was wrong. Dad finally told me the truth, that mother was not doing very well at all.

So I flew back home.

Mother was a different person. Not right away, but as time went by she began to dress rather slovenly. She had never been like that. She was always elegantly dressed, particularly when she was going to her Eastern Star meetings, where all the women wore beautiful gowns. But now she was on her way out. After a month or two, she began to wonder who Dad was. She felt that she was being forced to live in some strange place where she didn't belong.

Dad, later on, noticed that she was trying to force the lock on the door. She kept saying she wanted to go home.

We took her to the Hamilton General Hospital, and she was fairly comfortable for a short time. I wanted to stay with her as much as I could. I was with her day and night for several days. Then one day I decided I had to do a little bit of work in Toronto, and when I returned she had gone into a coma.

I held her warm hand for many hours with her eyes closed. And then she died. She was seventy-five.

PHOTOS

Opposite Foreword: Elizabeth Jean McFadden

Page 22: William McFadden (top) and David McFadden on the narrow-gauge train that runs from Ffestiniog to Porthmadog in northern Wales.

Page 26: Bill in the Lake District of England.

Page 29: Dave at the tomb of William Wordsworth, in the churchyard of the eleventh-century St. Oswald's in the Lake District.

Page 33: Dave at the ruins of a fourteenth-century church in Turso, on the northern tip of Scotland.

Page 35: Bill at the Isle of Mull.

Page 39: Dave and unidentified Welsh woman at the Skara Brae prehistoric settlement. on the Orkneys off the north coast of Scotland.

Page 49: Bill standing by Hadrian's Wall, just south of the Scotland-England border, near the town of Wall.

Page 69: Dave chats with a German solder who was visiting Vimy Ridge. He and his pal, also a German soldier, toured the Canadian tunnels with Dave and Bill.

Page 73: Dave at the Vimy monument erected by the Canadian government in 1936.

Page 76: Bill in front of the plaque commemorating the landing of the Royal Hamilton Light Infantry.

Page 87: Dave contemplates Stonehenge.

David W. McFadden has been publishing poetry
since the early 1960s. *Why Are You So Sad? Selected Poems of David W. McFadden* (Insomniac Press)
was shortlisted for the 2008 Griffin Prize for
Poetry, and *Be Calm, Honey* (Mansfield Press)
was shortlisted for the 2009 Governor General's
Award for Poetry (his third such nomination).
David is the author of about thirty books of poetry, fiction, and travel writing. He lives in Toronto.

Other books from Mansfield Press

Poetry

Leanne Averbach, *Fever*

Nelson Ball, *In This Thin Rain*

George Bowering, *Teeth: Poems 2006–2011*

Stephen Brockwell & Stuart Ross, eds., *Rogue Stimulus: The Stephen Harper Holiday Anthology for a Prorogued Parliament*

Diana Fitzgerald Bryden, *Learning Russian*

Alice Burdick, *Flutter*

Alice Burdick, *Holler*

Margaret Christakos, *wipe.under.a.love*

Pino Coluccio, *First Comes Love*

Gary Michael Dault, *The Milk of Birds*

Pier Giorgio Di Cicco, *The Dark Time of Angels*

Pier Giorgio Di Cicco, *Dead Men of the Fifties*

Pier Giorgio Di Cicco, *The Honeymoon Wilderness*

Pier Giorgio Di Cicco, *Living in Paradise*

Pier Giorgio Di Cicco, *Early Works*

Pier Giorgio Di Cicco, *The Visible World*

Salvatore Difalco, *What Happens at Canals*

Christopher Doda, *Aesthetics Lesson*

Christopher Doda, *Among Ruins*

Rishma Dunlop, *The Body of My Garden*

Rishma Dunlop, *Lover Through Departure: New and Selected Poems*

Rishma Dunlop, *Metropolis*

Rishma Dunlop & Priscila Uppal, eds., *Red Silk: An Anthology of South Asian Women Poets*

Ollivier Dyens, *The Profane Earth*

Jaime Forsythe, *Sympathy Loophole*

Carole Glasser Langille, *Late in a Slow Time*

Suzanne Hancock, *Another Name for Bridge*

Jason Heroux, *Emergency Hallelujah*

Jason Heroux, *Memoirs of an Alias*

Jason Heroux, *Natural Capital*

John B. Lee, *In the Terrible Weather of Guns*

Jeanette Lynes, *The Aging Cheerleader's Alphabet*

David W. McFadden, *Be Calm, Honey*

David W. McFadden, *What's the Score?*

Leigh Nash, *Goodbye, Ukulele*

Lillian Necakov, *The Bone Broker*

Lillian Necakov, *Hooligans*

Peter Norman, *At the Gates of the Theme Park*

Peter Norman, *Water Damage*

Natasha Nuhanovic, *Stray Dog Embassy*

Catherine Owen & Joe Rosenblatt, with Karen Moe, *Dog*

Corrado Paina, *The Alphabet of the Traveler*

Corrado Paina, *The Dowry of Education*

Corrado Paina, *Hoarse Legend*

Corrado Paina, *Souls in Plain Clothes*

Matt Santateresa. *A Beggar's Loom*

Matt Santateresa, *Icarus Redux*

Ann Shin, *The Last Thing Standing*

Jim Smith, *Back Off, Assassin! New and Selected Poems*

Jim Smith, *Happy Birthday, Nicanor Parra*

Robert Earl Stewart, *Campfire Radio Rhapsody*

Robert Earl Stewart, *Something Burned on the Southern Border*

Carey Toane, *The Crystal Palace*

Priscila Uppal, *Summer Sport: Poems*

Priscila Uppal, *Winter Sport: Poems*

Steve Venright, *Floors of Enduring Beauty*

Brian Wickers, *Stations of the Lost*

Fiction

Marianne Apostolides, *The Lucky Child*

Sarah Dearing, *The Art of Sufficient Conclusions*

Denis De Klerck, ed., *Particle & Wave: A Mansfield Omnibus of Electro-Magnetic Fiction*

Paula Eisenstein, *Flip Turn*

Marko Sijan, *Mongrel*

Tom Walmsley, *Dog Eat Rat*

Non-Fiction

George Bowering, *How I Wrote Certain of My Books*

Denis De Klerck & Corrado Paina, eds., *College Street–Little Italy: Toronto's Renaissance Strip*

Pier Giorgio Di Cicco, *Municipal Mind: Manifestos for the Creative City*

Amy Lavender Harris, *Imagining Toronto*

To order Mansfield Press titles online, please visit mansfieldpress.net